To Latrice,
You are a beautiful woman
who is truly loved
by the Almighty!
Love,
Laura
Lyn

Is She Dead Yet?

*The story of how a woman
struggled to escape domestic
violence and build a new life*

Lawanna Lynn Campbell

authorHOUSE®

AuthorHouse™
1663 Liberty Drive
Bloomington, IN 47403
www.authorhouse.com
Phone: 1-800-839-8640

First published by AuthorHouse   12/22/2009

ISBN: 978-1-4490-5496-0 (e)
ISBN: 978-1-4490-5497-7 (sc)

Printed in the United States of America
Bloomington, Indiana

This book is printed on acid-free paper.

To Christine, Jeff, and Michelle

The events described in this book are based on real incidents, but certain identifying details about some individuals have been changed.

All Holy Bible references are from the King James Version.

"We applaud your courage and bravery to relive your past in order to help someone else. Readers will find strength and discover the hope they never knew they had to free themselves from the grip of abuse. Your pain was not in vain." - Pastor Reginald & Linette Graham, Jesus Power & Love Ministries

"You really have a gift of telling your story in a way that I believe will be helpful to other women struggling in situations of domestic abuse. What I find most inspiring is that you've come to a place of finding love in your heart for the man who caused you so much pain." - Patricia Lavin, Clinical Social Worker

About the Book

Growing up with an alcoholic parent, Lawanna Lynn ("Lynn") walked on eggshells and learned to be submissive and codependent. She sought comfort and solace in Christianity and married at an early age. On the outside, Lynn and her husband were the perfect couple; but secretly, for nearly 23 years, she endured domestic violence that included rape and assault at the hands of her husband, who was also a business owner and church leader.

Join Lynn as she attempts to get help from some religious leaders who instead told her to keep silent about the abuse and his addiction to drugs and alcohol, extramarital affairs, and destructive behavior. Learn what she did right, what she did wrong, the warning signs of domestic abuse, and the five deadly marriage deal-breakers. Walk with her as she takes matters into her own hands and gets the legal, therapeutic, and spiritual help needed to make a new life for herself and build healthy relationships.

This poignant, true story will take you on a journey from the pulpit to the prison cell as Lynn strives to set herself free from a life of pain, shame, and guilt. Find out if she keeps the faith or if she turns away from God as she faces her most devastating challenge of all, and learn how you can also break the cycle of abuse. This gripping tale of a pastor's wife will keep you riveted to every word until the amazing surprise ending!

Contents

INTRODUCTION   xiii

PART I - THE BUILD UP

1	Early Warning Signs	3
2	Wedded Bliss	19
3	Let the Beatings Begin	29
4	Reconciliation	49
5	Five Deadly A's	57

PART II - THE BREAK DOWN

6	Wearing the Mask	69
7	One Boulder at a Time	79
8	Moving In	91
9	Time to Move Out	103
10	Feeling the Fear	117

PART III - BUILDING A NEW LIFE

11	Friends	127
12	In Therapy	135
13	A New Direction	147
14	Reflection: What Took Me So Long?	157
15	Residual Effects	171
Epilogue		181
Bibliography / Recommended Reading		185
About the Author		189

INTRODUCTION

One day a coworker asked me, "So, what's your story?"

Instantly, I was able to relate my experience with domestic abuse and tell him how I got out of it. My coworker marveled. He said that my story was worth telling and that I should find a platform. I tucked away his recommendation and put it on the back burner. That was five years ago.

***

My earliest recollection in life was when I was about five years of age. I sat by the living room window looking out on a rainy day wondering about God and where I came from. I daydreamed a lot and often thought about the meaning and significance of my life. I asked myself why I didn't remember being with God before I was born. I was pretty intense as a child and daydreamed a lot.

As a youngster, I enjoyed reading, poetry, coloring books, and storytelling, and during the summertime, I'd gather neighborhood children to play school. I had set up my family's basement into a mini classroom with a small chalkboard, tables, and chairs. I would pretend to be the teacher and would give the kids pencils, rulers, crayons, and ruled paper. I would stand at the chalkboard and teach basic writing and arithmetic. The parents didn't mind that I voluntarily took their little ones for an hour or so and babysat them at no charge, and I became a trusted teenager on the block.

I babysat and worked at a local dry cleaner, and by the time I was sixteen, in a pharmacy as a cashier and bookkeeper. In high school, I often wrote poems and short essays in my personal notebooks and for the school paper, and I excelled at schoolwork.

As an adult, my vivid imagination translated into great storytelling as I related Bible stories to children in a way that they could understand. I could captivate an audience with voice inflection and body movements that put the listener in the midst of the tale. I was often asked to speak at various events, such as presentations and lectures, or to serve as an emcee or mistress of ceremonies. My public speaking skills came naturally, and I don't ever recall shrinking from the stage.

***

In June 2007, a good friend of mine, who happened to be a pastor's wife, called me. She had been crying and was trying to hold back more tears as she told me about a couple in her church who had been in counseling with her and the pastor. Apparently, the husband had control issues and was very abusive to his wife. The wife had left her husband, and he had gone to her job early one morning before her shift started. He confronted her in the parking lot, and then shot and killed her. He sped off, and shortly thereafter, called his sons to tell them what he had done...and then he killed himself.

We both cried together on the phone. That event only intensified my sense of urgency to write this book. Many couples are struggling with domestic abuse and statistics show an increase in this devastating malady of society. However, many couples struggle in silence, and I discuss the reasons for this silence in a later chapter.

When I first moved to Long Island, I signed one of my daughters up for soccer and met another soccer mom during practice. She was a petite, frail woman who looked rather haggard. We became friends, and she eventually shared with me that she was separating from her abusive husband. At the time, she was on regular dialysis treatment going to the hospital several times a week because her husband beat her and damaged her kidneys. I listened intently to her as she recounted the horrors she had endured. I told her my story and encouraged her to continue her quest for emancipation. I also reassured her that she wasn't crazy for loving him in spite of everything and that she would leave the relationship on her terms and only when she was ready. She eventually pressed charges against her abuser, got a protective order, and filed for a divorce. Today, she is happy and healthy with two new babies, and in a loving relationship with a man who truly cares about her. And, the best news of all is that she no longer needs dialysis treatment.

Stories like these propelled me to write mine so that at least one precious woman can break free from domestic violence and find peace, love, and happiness.

Unfortunately though, we continue to hear stories in the news media which remind us that domestic violence is still prevalent and wreaking havoc in the lives of millions of people. Celebrities, prominent figures, and even religious leaders aren't spared the ugliness of this social issue and get top billing for it in magazine and newspaper articles. Web sites and blogs are filled with commentary and opinion about what should be done to the perpetrators, and sometimes they even blame the victims for provoking the abuse.

Seemingly, happy people commit horrendous crimes because they "snap" under the pressures of abuse. There are a few television programs, talk shows, and movies, like *Snapped*, *The Burning Bed*, *Enough*, and *What's Love Got to Do with It*, which tell the stories of women affected by domestic violence. The psychological trauma and residual effects are tearing our families apart, and people are being maimed or murdered at the hands of an intimate partner.

***

You're probably asking yourself what professional expertise or authority I have with domestic abuse, and how it relates to being a pastor's wife. You're probably wondering if this is a book about religion or if I'll be preaching in it. You want to know why I stayed as long as I did and how I eventually escaped.

This book is not about religion. Domestic abuse is not a respecter of persons. It wreaks havoc on all of us regardless of age, economic status, race, religion, nationality, or educational background. I don't have the luxury to preach from a platform when so many women are dying regardless of their "religion." Let me be clear. Do you reach for the hand of a drowning man and ask him what religion he is before you pull him up? I don't.

This book is about love and relationships and my desire to be loved at any cost. This is a story about my struggle with accepting and forgiving myself and others. I was a victim of domestic abuse by a man I loved dearly, who also served as a pastor for a short while. I survived the abuse and am writing to help other women who are suffering in silence.

As a pastor's wife, I understood the pressures of managing a church and its members. What makes my story a little special is that I not only had to deal with the abuse and other marital issues that compounded the problem, but also had to incorporate church doctrine and Biblical principles into my decision-making process. I asked myself whether I should forgive or retaliate -- reconcile or divorce -- love or hate. I eventually learned how to pack and pray and was able to separate my two identities -- one as a woman and one as a pastor's wife -- and incorporate both approaches from the legal and Biblical points of view.

***

I'm a goal-oriented individual, and for the past 15 years, I have made a list of goals for myself at the beginning of each year. Some of the goals repeated into the following year or the next, or a goal would be revised and restated. There were a few that were never fulfilled, and I decided that those goals were either not realistic or unattainable, and I discarded them.

If a goal made it to the list, then I was determined to get it accomplished. So, I was very careful about what I wrote. I only listed goals that I knew I could achieve or at least goals that were in reach and could be attained over time. Goals that seemed out of reach never made it to my journal. Dreams and desires for a perfect life were relegated to a "wish" list that was kept on a piece of paper somewhere in the bottom of my nightstand drawer, never to be seen again!

In October 2007, my personal coach asked me to list my short- and long-term goals. When I listed "writing a book" as a long-term goal, I immediately became aware that this was something I had to do. I had always talked about it but had never written it down before then. Once it was printed on a piece of paper, it became real for me.

I had committed myself to writing down the day's events in a journal at the urging of my marriage therapist over ten years ago. I had also taken a time management and financial planning seminar at work that encouraged personal journaling in order to identify spending habits and obstacles to financial success. I continued the practice and had immediate results, but I also identified some shortcomings.

It was my old notes and journals that helped me in the long run. I was able to recall dates and times of significant events, as well as pinpoint critical mistakes that perpetuated the cycle of abuse that I had experienced. I encourage you to journey with me as I learned how to break that cycle of abuse and move toward a relatively normal way of living.

While writing this book, I had sleepless nights and plenty of solitude. I declined invitations to dinner, club meetings, special events, and movies. Sometimes, I even forgot to eat a meal because I was so engrossed in putting my thoughts into print. There were times when I had to stop writing because life was still happening around me. My daughter needed me for high school and college events, I needed to complete other projects, or I needed to go to my full-time job and earn a living.

Sometimes I'd cry at the keyboard because it hurt so much to relive those awful moments, and it would take days before I could go back to the computer and continue where I left off. There were times when my sleep was interrupted because I would have a thought or idea that needed to be recorded immediately. I kept a notepad and pen on the nightstand. There were also times, when I could not ignore the nagging feeling that I had missed something and would go back and rewrite. But eventually, I came to the end of the task and was able to finish this project. My goal of writing a book was complete, and I could draw a line through that item in my journal.

***

The book is divided into three parts. Part I covers part of my teen years, the early years of my marriage and the evolution of our relationship. Part II covers the breakdown of the marriage and presents the steps I took towards ending the violence. Part III discusses the reasons why I stayed, why it took me so long to leave, and the negative impact of domestic violence and divorce on our family. I'll talk facts and figures about the economic impact on our health system, the sexual assaults, stalking, homicide, injury, and its effect on our children who witness such atrocities.

I attempt to be gentle for the sake of my children, but the reality of our lives back then and today is anything but. I ask my children to forgive me for putting them through that experience at a price they could not afford to pay.

It is my hope that as you read my story, you're propelled into action to help someone you know who's going through domestic violence. You may even see yourself in these pages and will take steps to end the maddening cycle of abuse. There may be situations that you weren't even aware of as abuse that are mentioned here. It is my prayer that you love yourself enough to save yourself and any children you may have, or that you love your mother, sister, aunt, niece, cousin, coworker, or choir member enough to say something to encourage them. May God help you and may He put people in your life to help guide you through the muddy waters to the surface where you can breathe clean, fresh air.

And one day when someone asks you, "So, what's your story?" you'll have an answer.

PART I
THE BUILD UP

1
Early Warning Signs

*"When I was a child, I spake as a child, I understood as a child,
I thought as a child: but when I became a man,
I put away childish things." – 1 Corinthians 13:11*

It was the end of summer 1974 and the beginning of my high school senior year. I climbed into the back seat of my friend's car and sat next to another kid who was going to a party with us. His name was Kevin, and he was a couple of years younger than me, slim and cute with chocolate-colored skin and a big Afro that swayed in the wind as it swirled around us. I knew he'd ask me to braid his hair one day. It had become the trend, and I was popular for my hair-braiding skills. A few days later, while I was in his family's basement braiding his hair into cornrows, someone peeped down the stairs and yelled, "Who's that?"

I looked up at another bushy-headed young man who wore small, round, wire-rimmed glasses. His name was Jeffery, and he was a lot taller than his younger brother, skinny and very handsome, and his skin complexion was much lighter than his brother's. I thought for sure my friend was adopted because both of his parents were very light-skinned, and he had often referred to himself as the black sheep of the family. The three of us played pool and drank sodas in the basement, and by the end of the evening I came to realize that they were indeed biological brothers.

I later found out that the two brothers made some sort of deal or bet about me, and I guess Jeff won. He began calling me on the phone regularly, and we would talk for hours. Soon we started going out on dates and frequently went to our favorite restaurant in Center City, where we'd have a delicious steak dinner with a tossed salad, baked potato, and garlic bread. He spared no expense, and I enjoyed the lavish treatment and the special attention that he showered on me. Within two months of our initial meeting, I was infatuated and slept with him.

I counted the days on the calendar that hung on my bedroom wall. 27-28-29-30-31-32-33. My period should have come already. "I can't be pregnant," I mumbled. "I just can't be pregnant," I repeated with increased agitation. "I'm going to college." My voice trailed as my eyes began to tear. Within weeks, on a cold, gray day in December, my eyes would water again.

My mother and I took a long train ride to a suburban clinic in another county. The bare, brown trees that lined the train tracks somberly watched the train cars pass by. It felt like the trees were standing guard over the rails, stepping aside to allow passage into some forbidden land. The train rattled and rolled along, stopping and hissing occasionally to let passengers on and off. This wasn't the inner city. This wasn't the projects or the ghetto. It was some faraway place where people go when they don't want to be recognized. I didn't want to make eye contact with anyone, so I looked out the window and stared at the trees. My breath hit the window, and the fog clouded my view, but it didn't disguise this journey that would change my life. I suspected that the guardian trees and everybody else on the train knew where I was going and what I was planning to do that day. Even though no one looked directly at me, my paranoia filled in the blanks and I believed that everyone knew I was hiding a shameful secret. The shame and guilt I felt that day would come back to haunt me and stay with me for a very long time.

When we arrived at the women's medical center, I noticed a definite change in my surroundings. The clean and sterile waiting area had pastel colored walls, arrangements of assorted plastic flowers on the tables and neatly arranged women's magazines. It was a big improvement from the dark and dismal train ride in slate- and gray-colored structures. There was a warm and welcome feeling in the air -- not at all like the impersonal, cold streets of the inner city.

A few other teenage girls and young women were already in the reception area, and we all sat quietly, each paired with her companion for the procedure -- a mother, a female relative, a boyfriend, or a girlfriend. They would take us home, hold us if we cried or lost our composure, or maybe just make sure that the deed was done so they could breathe a sigh of relief, knowing that they would not be engulfed by the shame we would have brought on our families. Taking me to a place so far out of town ensured that no one in our neighborhood or in our family would ever know that I got pregnant and had an abortion. And the secret would be kept safe.

My mother made the arrangements, and, since I was still a minor, she had to fill out the paperwork. I was ashamed about the whole thing and sat quietly. I didn't want to cause any more problems or make matters worse by protesting. I had already disappointed my mother and my father, and surely, what I had done put a strain on their already fragile marriage. How could I have been so careless and gotten pregnant? I didn't want to have an abortion, but I had no choice. My mother insisted that it be done. I was going to college, and she wouldn't allow my future to be derailed because of some boy. All I could think about was how I could ever live with myself.

A few of us were called into another room, where chairs were arranged in a semicircle. As we took a seat it was obvious that this was going to be some kind of therapy session. A social worker sat among us and asked how we were feeling and if we knew what was going to happen to us. She gave us pamphlets about the female reproductive system, pregnancy, abortion, our rights, and the risks. She told us about the procedure and what we could expect. She explained what emotions we could expect to have and how long it would take our bodies to get back to normal. We were going to take confirming pregnancy tests, get examined, and be prepped. I thought that I would never be normal after this day. I wished I could have stood up for myself and for my baby and just walked out. I wished I could've screamed and yelled at my mother for making me do something that I didn't want to do and what I knew God did not like. But I just sat there. Quietly.

We were called one-by-one into an examining room, and when my name was called, I was obedient and did as I was instructed. I was already prepped and had taken the pill I was given to ease the anxiety. Now dressed in the cloth green gown, I sat waiting on the edge of the examining table. The nurse came in and fussed about in the cold room. I was guided to lie down on the death bed of my baby, covered myself from the waist down in a lightweight sheet, and put my feet in the icy stirrups. My body began to tremble. I could feel the heat from the lamp that was aimed at my lower body, and as the intravenous drip was being set up, my eyes began to water.

The middle-aged doctor came in, and two nurses began to scurry about in the room. The doctor examined me. The pressure of his probing made me uneasy, and when he inserted the speculum I began to shake even more. The room seemed to get colder, and all of a sudden I felt like I was dozing off. As I tried to think about other things, I heard the suction sound of a vacuum cleaner. I could feel the hose brushing against one of my legs. Tears began to fall down the sides of my face, and one of the nurses held my hand and tried to soothe me. I was shaking and trembling. It was so cold in that room. I couldn't stop shaking, and I couldn't stop the tears from falling. But I was going to be brave and didn't make a sound. As I started to drift off into a light sleep, all I heard and thought about was the vacuum cleaner shredding the limbs of my baby. I began to cry deep within and let out only a whimper. I thought, "God will never forgive me for this."

I don't remember the trip home.

Later that evening I was lying on the couch praying that the cramps would go away. I tried to sleep and rest as I was instructed to do. Jeff knew that I had the abortion that day and came over to see me. He sat down at the other end of the couch. He peeked into the brown paper bag that sat on the floor beside the couch. In it was a large box of Kotex sanitary napkins. He was embarrassed and looked apologetic for being so nosy. He said that he was sorry I was in so much pain. I told him that I didn't like what I had done. He said I should have told him and that he would've argued with my mother on my behalf. He said he hadn't wanted the abortion either and was looking forward to a kid. I had only known him for four months and had no idea he was willing to help me raise a baby. I wasn't sure that I was even ready for that assignment. But it was too late now.

I never talked about the abortion again after that. Not with anyone.

***

It was time to buckle down and concentrate on schoolwork. My mom and dad were pretty adamant that I not be involved with Jeff anymore, and my father even issued the edict, "That's it. No more sex!" But, I still saw him, and one morning I cut school to go see him. He lived with his elderly aunt who lived in the next block from Jeff's parent's home. Since she used a walker and lived mostly in the living room, Jeff had helped her with household chores and errands. She was a sweet old woman who loved to talk. This morning, though, I didn't stop to chitchat with her as I used to and ran upstairs. I was sitting in a chair by the window in Jeff's bedroom with my school books on my lap when the phone rang. I watched as Jeff's expression changed from his usual charming smile to a deep frown. It was my mom on the other end. She asked him if I was there. Jeff denied it. She demanded that he put me on the phone, and he pointed it in my direction.

The principal had called the house looking for me, since I had not shown up at school. He wanted to hear the speech I had prepared for an upcoming debate presentation and had made an announcement over the loud speakers that was heard in every classroom. When I didn't respond, the teachers and administrators did an all-out search. They called the police because they thought I had been abducted on my way to school. No one thought I could have actually cut school, because that wasn't like me. When the principal called the house to report that I was missing, my mom knew instantly that I had gone to be with Jeff. She found my phone book and looked up Jeff's number. I took the phone and listened as my mother yelled and screamed and threatened. And then I picked up my books and went home. I was on punishment.

When I returned to school the next day, I told the principal and teachers that I had an appointment that I had forgotten to tell my mom about. My classmates teased me, because there was a rumor going around that I cut school to be with my boyfriend. One of my classmates said that she didn't believe the rumors, that she knew I wouldn't do anything like that, and that I was way too smart for that kind of thing. Inwardly, I cringed and was sorry for disappointing her.

The rest of my senior year was exciting. I loved school and was looking forward to college. I thought about going away to school and completed several in-state college applications. Since we were a poor family, I could only go to the school that offered the most financial aid. I received a Meritorious Scholarship Award for outstanding academic performance from the Philadelphia Board of Education and was accepted into Temple University. The award was a full four-year scholarship.

I was ecstatic, and my family was proud. My parents beamed as they bragged to their friends and family that their oldest daughter was going to college. I would commute to school, since Temple was only six blocks from my house. And now that college admission was all wrapped up, I saw no need to continue to work at getting superior grades. I decided not to complete a specific class project, and my Social Sciences grade slid down to a "B." I maintained my overall "A" average in the other classes, even though I had not put forth much effort. I continued working my after-school job as a pharmacy cashier and billing clerk and enjoyed having the extra cash.

Jeff escorted me to the prom and attended the graduation ceremony with the rest of my family. Throughout the summer we'd occasionally take a bus ride to visit his relatives. His family allowed him to drink beer and other forms of alcohol, and sometimes he would go out of sight and come back smelling like marijuana. I could tell he was trying to hide this from me, but I suspected that something else might be going on. On a visit to his friend's apartment, he told me that he occasionally used intravenous drugs, but was going to stop because of me. He said he knew I didn't like it. Since he had stopped smoking cigarettes earlier that year, I knew that he had the willpower and determination to break this habit, too. I believed in him, and he stopped shooting up. I saw the changes he made for me, and I was not willing to give up on him yet, especially since he was good to me.

***

One day in late July while we were on the phone talking, he asked me about other guys I had dated since knowing him. I wasn't prepared for the question. I suspected he was not a one-woman man and that he had been sleeping with other girls -- one in particular. Once, when I went to see him at his aunt's house, he wouldn't answer the door. Instead, he leaned out of the upstairs window and told me that he couldn't come out because he was busy. I knew that the other girl was up there. The plain-looking, full-bodied, light-skinned one. I saw Jeff talking with her once before, and she had that "round-the-way" girl look -- you know, the look of the girls in your neighborhood who are rumored to sleep around. And her complexion was so light that she could pass for white. She had the upper hand and I was jealous. I had been teased by other kids about my dark skin, and I had not yet accepted the "Black is Beautiful" mantra.

Isn't it amazing how Black people would describe other Black people by first indicating their shades or hues? Light skinned. Dark skinned. Brown skinned. High yella. Or just plain ole blue black. And the next most important descriptor would be hair texture. Good hair or nappy hair. Someone with good hair must've been of Indian or some other racial background. I grew up believing that being dark-skinned was bad. I grew up believing that having nappy hair was bad. So, in my mind, I already had two strikes against me.

I began to sweat and started thinking about how I could tell him about Freddie. I wanted to be honest with him and not be called a liar later on. It was best to get it out in the open now, so that if anything unpleasant went down I could get out without investing any more time into this relationship. So, I told him about Freddie, whom I had been seeing off and on just before meeting Jeff. There was dead silence on the other end of the line. Then all of a sudden I heard the high-pitched crashing ring sound that a phone makes when it's slammed down or slammed against a wall. I could feel my underarms tingling and perspiration beading on my skin, and without a word I gently eased the phone down in its cradle. He didn't call back. I didn't call him either. I was too scared.

A few days later, Jeff called me. He said that he forgave me and wanted to see me. I thought, "Forgave me? Forgave me for what?" There wasn't anything to forgive. So, I skipped over. We only lived a few blocks away from each other, and if I stood at the end of my street and looked as far as I could, I could see him at the corner of his street.

We sat on the bed, and he asked me about the details of my relationship with Freddie, so, I explained as calmly and clearly as I could. He listened intently and then without warning lunged for my throat and started choking me. His grip was tight, and I squirmed and began gasping for air. As he pressed hard against my neck, I could actually feel my eyes bulge and the veins protrude at my temples. His eyes seemed to pierce right through me. I couldn't scream. As suddenly as he had pounced on me, he released his hold. I inhaled deeply and began coughing.

My eyes began to tear. I was trying to figure out what had just happened when he then pulled me to him and started hugging me and kissing me and apologizing. He started moaning and crying and saying how sorry he was for choking me and that he loved me. I was confused. He loves me? He held onto me for a long time as though I would disappear if he let me go. As we lay on the bed exhausted from the physical and emotional ordeal, he continued to hold me tight, apologizing over and over, rubbing my hair and face, and kissing me gently. I must've fallen asleep. I didn't notice the scratches and bruises on my neck until the next day. My mother noticed them, too. She and my aunt confronted me and asked me what had happened between us that caused him to go for my neck. I told them that he was jealous over some other guy and left it at that. They left it at that as well.

Over the next few weeks, Jeff made concerted efforts to show how remorseful he was, and I accepted his apology. I attributed his fit of rage to his loving me so much. One night we were watching *Saturday Night Live* at his parents' house. His mom was upstairs, his father was out drinking, and the house was quiet and dark except for the flickering TV screen. We laughed at Eddie Murphy in the foam Gumby suit smoking a cigar and talking with a Jewish accent, and we snuggled in each other's arms lying on the floor by the couch. I could tell Jeff wanted sex, but I was uncomfortable about it and rejected his advances. His brother walked into the house and went into the kitchen.

I could feel Jeff's body tense, and he turned over and positioned himself over me. He didn't say a word, but I knew that something bad was about to happen. In one swift movement, he pinned my arms over my head and straddled me like a horse. His weight was crushing, and I couldn't move. As I tried to twist myself out from under his grip, he spat on me and then just stared at me, daring me to scream or yell or cry out. He was breathing fast. The spittle had landed between my right cheek and the side of my nose and had started to ooze. Fortunately, the slime didn't get into my mouth or eyes, which were tightly shut. I didn't say a word. I just clenched my teeth. He got up and went into the kitchen with his brother. I could hear Jeff talking and laughing with his brother as if nothing had happened. I wiped the spit off my face, got up, and left.

The next morning, I went to church as usual. Jeff called that afternoon and apologized for spitting in my face the night before. He was determined to prove that everything would be all right between us and had promised that he'd make it up to me. He told me he had a surprise for me and offered to take me shopping for school clothes. I was hesitant but agreed to go. The next day, as I fingered the rack of leather jackets in a downtown department store, he eagerly picked out one my size and proceeded to the checkout counter to buy it. I objected. He knew that I liked the jacket and that I couldn't afford it. He repeatedly presented this gift as a token of his appreciation, but I still would not accept it. When I later told my mother that he wanted to buy the coat for me, she ridiculed me for not accepting it and told me that I must've been crazy to let a leather jacket slip out of my hands. She didn't know that he had spit in my face only a few days before.

***

In his efforts to please me, Jeff volunteered to go to church with me one Sunday. He had no previous religious exposure. I was intrigued by his gesture to join me in something that was so foreign to him. I also thought this would be a step in the right direction and accepted his peace offering.

I had been attending one particular Baptist church since I was 13. When I was younger, our family attended my grandfather's church where he was a deacon. I don't ever remember my father going to church with us though. On Sunday afternoons after church, we'd go back to my grandparents' home for family dinners with my aunts, uncles, and cousins. The adults would sit at the dining room table, and the children would sit at a much smaller table in the kitchen. We all feasted on fried chicken, biscuits, macaroni and cheese, rice and gravy, string beans, collard greens, and, of course, Kool-aid. During the summer after dinner, we would run and play outside until dusk. My dress and white ankle socks would always get dirty, and my black patent leather shoes would always get scuffed. Truly, those summer Sunday afternoons with family were the best days of my childhood.

But when we became teenagers, the Sunday tradition faded. I was the only one in my immediate family who went to church regularly. I had already outgrown the junior choir and was now serving as the Sunday School secretary. My duties were to record Sunday School class attendance and that morning's offering, as well as read the minutes from the prior Sunday's activities. There were strict procedures at the church, and I followed them faithfully. Bible classes were taught in a room across from the main sanctuary and were completed just before the 11 o'clock worship services. Jeff was impressed that I had such an important position at such a young age. I took it in stride. I had been doing the job for a couple of years then and was well respected among the congregation.

I noticed that Jeff occasionally displayed keen spiritual insight and that he was quick to point out inconsistencies with certain religious rituals at my church. Once when he was stopped at the front door of the church by one of the deacons who questioned him about not wearing a tie, Jeff said that he didn't have one. The deacon insisted that he buy one and wear it the next time. Jeff remarked that he didn't think Jesus would mind if he came without one, so why should the deacon object. I agreed. It was these moments of revelation and clear perception that led me to believe that Jeff was headed towards greatness. He wasn't afraid to challenge the status quo, and I admired that.

***

College coursework began, and my schedule was intense. I didn't realize how difficult it was going to be to make the transition from high school to college, and I felt ill-prepared. My advisor was a very senior member of the faculty staff and looked as though she should have retired years ago. My courses included accounting, psychology, philosophy, reading, science, and science lab. Even though I had done quite well in high school, I was floundering in accounting and barely passing in science. I did, however, enjoy the smaller classroom settings for my philosophy and reading courses and did extremely well in those courses.

I would call Jeff from a pay phone and complain about how overwhelmed I felt. Sitting in the large auditorium and lecture halls intimidated me. I met a few other struggling freshmen along the way who also complained about that sense of isolation. I just couldn't adjust to the enormous campus and most of the time felt lost. My mind wandered a lot, and I didn't feel like I fit in. I had pretty much made up in my mind that college wasn't for me, but I still got up everyday and went to class.

***

My uncle, who I heard had gotten "saved," had invited Jeff and me to visit his church during revival services. I wasn't too keen about going to my uncle's church. He had turned into a "holy roller" after years of wild living, and I viewed Pentecostals as religious fanatics. They would jump up and down in church, dancing and shouting, falling out in the "spirit," and talking in some strange language. It was called "speaking in tongues." I thought it was very strange and that maybe these people were possessed or something. My Baptist church was quiet and reserved, and everything was done in an orderly fashion. Jeff didn't know anything about the different denominations within Christianity and was excited about going to visit another church. So I agreed to go.

We walked into the huge foyer of the church, which used to be a movie theater back in the 1960's. It was renovated and purchased by Reverend Benjamin Smith and was now a spiritual haven where hundreds gathered to worship and praise God. I was accustomed to a small church setting and was mesmerized by the size and seating capacity of the theater. The church was filled with people on that Friday night. The usher led us to seats on the second row, front and center where my uncle was waiting. He had held two seats for us and greeted us warmly. I had never seen my mother's brother so happy.

Jeff and I were awestruck. The music was lively, and people were singing all around us. The praise and worship leader enthusiastically encouraged people to sing along as he taught the lyrics. There was a pianist, a drummer, and a guitar player whose musical chords blasted through the amplifiers and speakers around the auditorium. It was electrifying, and the energy was contagious. Worshippers were clapping and singing joyously to the upbeat songs. You could feel the excitement in the atmosphere. My heart raced, and it was no time at all before we fell into the charismatic sing-along with the congregation. This was nothing like the Baptist church, where we sang from hymnals as chords from the organ filled the air.

The minister stirred our hearts even more. His fiery preaching about hell and damnation convicted me, and within moments I became aware of the sin in my life and felt guilty. I dismissed the feeling of guilt because I was already a member of a church and felt pretty "safe." Yet I had never before felt such a tugging on my heart. I thought that surely I wasn't a sinner. I had never hurt anyone. But then I remembered that I had committed murder by having the abortion and felt deep remorse. I tried to brush it off and not allow this stranger shouting from the stage to brainwash me and make me go down to the altar. I thought to myself that I was going to look all this stuff up in the Bible when I got home. I just couldn't get it out of my mind. Does the Bible really say that I'm going to Hell? I raised my hands, started to cry, and went down to the altar so the preacher could lay hands on me and pray for me. Jeff was already at the altar.

Within the next few days after our experience at my uncle's church, Jeff told me that he was tired of his life and wanted a change. He wanted to get rid of the feelings of anxiety and fear and asked me how he could get "saved." He had been pondering what had happened during the revival meeting. Since I had been going to church since I was young, he knew that I would know how to get saved. I prayed with him over the phone the words that I had been taught. I believed the words of the prayer but knew that I had not fully given up all to follow Jesus. I was going to church on Sundays, but doing my own thing on Mondays, Tuesdays, and the other days of the week. Something was missing, and I needed a change as well. And as I recited those familiar words, my faith was renewed. Jeff accepted Christ that night over the phone and began his quest for spiritual development.

Shortly after that, we started regularly attending my uncle's church. One Sunday afternoon, Jeff joined my uncle's church, and that evening he had a lot of questions and wanted to go over the Bible scriptures with me. We recalled what the pastor had read in 1 Corinthians 7:9, "But if they cannot contain, let them marry: for it is better to marry than to burn."

We felt guilty about our sins and didn't want to burn in hell because of them. We wanted to please God and live right. The consequences of continuing in sin were death, eternal separation from the Lord, and burning in the lake of fire. Based on our incorrect interpretation of that Bible verse and our own naivety, we thought that it was better to marry each other than to burn in hell and be condemned for committing sexual sin. So, without hesitation, Jeff asked me to marry him. I loved him and believed getting married would be the right thing to do. I agreed, and we set a date -- November 8...and I was only 18 years old.

***

Reflections:

1. The correct interpretation for 1 Corinthians 7:9 is that it is better to marry than to burn in your own sexual lusts and desires, not to burn in the lake of fire as we first thought. At the time, we acted on what we believed was correct, and years later, we learned the true meaning of that Scripture.
2. Familiarize yourself with the symptoms of dating violence.
3. Determine if you suffer from post-abortion syndrome.
4. Learn how your family of origin influences your decisions as a young adult.
5. Low self-image made me vulnerable to unhealthy relationships.

2
Wedded Bliss

"Therefore shall a man leave his father and his mother, and shall cleave unto his wife: and they shall be one flesh."
— Genesis 2:24

My mother expressed her objection to my getting married right from the start, but she eventually conceded anyway. She said that I was old enough to make my own decision and that she wouldn't stand in the way. I never understood why she didn't insist that I not marry him. I don't recall my father having any comment except that he just wanted me to be happy.

Planning the wedding seemed easy. I used the residual college scholarship money to pay for the flowers and the rings. Jeff had been laid off from his job at the food distribution center and was still collecting unemployment benefits, so money for him was tight. We hadn't made big plans for the ceremony or for a honeymoon. By this time, he had already purchased his first suit since he was going to church regularly, and my prom dress would do double duty as a wedding gown. It was a soft white polyester A-line halter gown with an Empire-style jacket. We got married at my Baptist church. We didn't feel comfortable asking to use my uncle's church, because the pastor didn't even know us. It was raining when I woke up that morning, and I hoped that the bad weather wasn't a sign of what my marriage would be. By early afternoon, the rain stopped, and the sun was shining. It was unseasonably warm that November day, and we didn't need overcoats or jackets.

When I arrived at the church, I realized that I had forgotten to ask someone to play the piano at the ceremony. I left the waiting room and ran down the aisle to ask Mrs. Jones to play, and as she eagerly agreed, someone whisked me away, saying it was bad luck for the bride to be seen before the ceremony. Oops. I had forgotten about that rule, too.

The actual ceremony was short and sweet with no major flubs, except when Jeff jumped the gun (not the broom as done in the African tradition) and answered "I do" instead of waiting for the instruction to say "I will." I guess he wanted to marry me so badly he just couldn't wait. We smiled at his eagerness and at each other. When we kissed after the minister pronounced us man and wife, a drunken stranger staggered down the center aisle, got right up to me, and asked if he could kiss the bride. I was stunned. I thought, "Where did this man come from? Who is he and how did he get far enough down the aisle to accost us without anyone intercepting him?" Just then, my brother burst into the sanctuary with leftover streamers in one hand, totally surprised that he had missed the entire ceremony. He had been outside decorating the guests' cars with crepe paper the whole time, and no one went to tell him that the ceremony had started.

My aunt Lorraine offered her home for the reception because we couldn't afford a banquet hall and catering. On our way there, we stopped to see Jeff's mom. She had not attended the wedding, because she suffered from agoraphobia and rarely ventured outside her home. Things just weren't working out the way I thought they would on such a special day. But by that time, I had resigned all expectations for smooth sailing and had accepted that "*the best laid plans of mice and men often go awry.*" Not only did the day start off with rain, but I was seen before the ceremony started, my brother and mother-in-law both missed the ceremony, and a total drunken stranger crashed the event. I thought, "What else could be in store for us?"

***

Jeff was on fire for God, and his excitement was infectious. I moved in with Jeff at his aunt's home, and we went to church every Sunday morning and Wednesday evening. Jeff went to Friday night prayer services, which usually lasted all through the night, and helped man the church phone lines. Distressed people called the church for prayer and advice, and with guidance from senior level ministers, Jeff would be there to answer their calls. My uncle Coleman got Jeff a job at the candy factory, and the two would go to work together. They would talk to coworkers about Jesus and were considered an unbeatable force at winning new converts for the Lord. I beamed with pride as my zealous husband told stories about the day's and night's victories. But with this newfound faith came some pretty big changes.

Within weeks, my husband started to dictate how I should dress and insisted that I stop taking birth control. He started quoting verses from the Bible that talked about how a woman should adorn herself and not wear anything pertaining to a man. The church leadership had cautioned women not to wear pants. I protested but didn't want to make my husband feel less than a man, so I consented to wearing only skirts and dresses. I remembered thumbing through the small portable closet and pointing out to him that most of my wardrobe consisted of pantsuits, slacks, and jeans. I gave in nonetheless.

The issue of birth control annoyed me. I stressed to him that for me to stop taking birth control pills would surely bring children into the marriage well before we were financially able to care for them. He insisted that the Lord would take care of us. Now, I was getting nervous. I loved Jeff and did want children, but not so soon.

The excitement of wedded bliss caused my concentration in schoolwork to wane, and I decided that I had bigger concerns than my education. I was married now and needed to concentrate on being a good wife and starting a family. So at the end of my first semester at Temple University, I quit college – a decision that I would regret for the rest of my life. By the end of January 1976, I had a new job and found out that I was pregnant.

Our families were excited about the baby and hosted a baby shower for us that summer. There were a few unmarried pregnant friends and family members attending the shower, and a tinge of self-righteousness rose up in me. I felt a little superior to them because I was married and they were not. But as soon as the thought took hold, I remembered that I had committed the unthinkable not that long ago. I immediately became ashamed and looked at these brave women as wonderful and beautiful for not allowing the stigma of being an unwed mother to stop them from bringing another human being into the world. They had decided that their baby was more important than anything else. They had been more courageous than I could ever be. I felt depraved and full of self-hatred and self-loathing. How could I ever make up for what I had done? I then looked at unwed mothers in a new way – as loving and beautiful women. I was nothing like that.

***

It was a Wednesday morning when my water broke, and my aunt drove me to the hospital. I called Jeff at work, and he rushed to the hospital just in time to wait for what would be a long 21 hours. By the next morning I still had not delivered, and we were told that a C-section would be performed. Jeff and I did not want to have that procedure and began praying that it would not have to be done. I intensified my panting and breathing techniques, and at 10:07 Thursday morning, a healthy baby girl was born. As her tiny bluish-gray body began to take color, Jeff and I looked at each other and in unison expressed awe, wonder, and amazement. It was September 2, 1976, and Christine Louise made her debut. Our beautiful baby girl came into this world just five days after the predicted due date.

As I was being wheeled out of the delivery room to recovery, the nurses laughed and shouted, "See you next year." In a weakened chuckle, I said, "Oh, no you won't."

I went back to work after six weeks, and my mom took care of Christine. Jeff and I had settled into a routine, and he continued to attend the weekly Bible study classes and services. I enjoyed being a mother and meticulously cared for our baby. I felt blessed to have a healthy child and vowed do my best to protect and nurture this gift from God. The Bible says in Psalms 127:3, "Lo, children *are* an heritage of the LORD: *and* the fruit of the womb *is his* reward." Part of this recognition of God's favor would be having Christine dedicated. The Christening was scheduled, and to my delight my father came to church to witness the ceremony. You see, my father had only attended church once in my memory, and that was during my wedding. It didn't bother me that he arrived at church late and a little intoxicated. I had already forgiven him by the time he sat down beside us that Sunday afternoon.

My father used to tell the story about the time he left me alone on the couch when I was just months old. My mother left me in his care one afternoon, and all I did was cry. Daddy told me that he changed my diaper, fed me a bottle, and walked me around the small house but that I continued to cry. There was nothing he could do to stop the crying, and he couldn't tolerate the noise. He said he laid me on the couch, propped pillows all around me, and went outside. I continued to cry and scream as he stood outside smoking a cigarette. I fondly remembered that story, but somehow I felt that he had abandoned me and felt that, if he were confronted with some difficult task, he would run from it. Maybe that's why I had pity on him and accepted his alcoholism. I had come to realize that it was his way to escape some painful reality that he could not control.

***

I kept dozing off at my desk at work and my boss started to tease that I was pregnant again. I laughed it off but later found out that he was right. The neonatal nurses at Pennsylvania Hospital were right, too. They told me that I would be back again next year. How right they were. I was put on bed rest for a few weeks during my first trimester because of complications and was cleared to go back to work after the bleeding stopped. Then my husband told me that we were moving.

"Moving?" I was surprised at his announcement and didn't have any idea that he had already made arrangements.

"We're moving in with your uncle," he said flatly.

Within days, he had packed all of our belongings, and we moved to another part of town with my uncle, his wife, and their two daughters. We placed our meager possessions in a box in one corner of the bedroom that would be home for the next few months. My commute to work on public transportation was longer than before, and as my pregnancy progressed, I grew weary of carrying the load and walking long distances between the bus stop and my uncle's home.

Months before, Jeff had begged me to let him buy a used car with the proceeds of a trust fund that held the financial settlement from his childhood accident with a city trash truck. The trust was paid out when Jeff turned 21, and I recommended that we save it for a home or use it to move into an apartment of our own. But he got down on bended knee at the used car dealership, pleading his case to have that car. That's how he learned so much about cars and auto repairs. That used car broke down more times than it ran. So while he and Uncle Coleman drove up the boulevard to work every day, I hauled my fat butt to the bus stop. Sometimes, though, I was able to get a ride home with a coworker.

I enjoyed my job as an intake secretary at the state employment office, where I helped people on welfare find jobs. I was part of the interview team, which had great working relationships. We would have lunch together and go to each other's homes for special occasions like birthday parties and baby showers. We'd have lively discussions and debates about Christianity. One man was Catholic, and he constantly had questions about the Trinity.

One woman, Maxine Barfield, didn't believe in God at all. She was soft spoken and patient, with a pleasant demeanor. She was married but didn't have any children. Somehow, though, we developed a close friendship, and I would talk to her about my relationship with God during our lunch hours together. She'd ask questions, and I'd answer them the best way I could. I'd bring in little pocket-sized booklets called tracks that I got from church and would share them with her. I had just turned 20. I was on fire for the Lord, too, and wanted to tell the world about how good God was.

Maxine offered to drive me to and from work, and it was during one of those drives that I invited her to visit our church. She did come one Sunday and left abruptly when she couldn't find me in the sanctuary. But she eventually came back, heard the message of salvation, and accepted Jesus Christ as her personal Lord and Savior. We became even closer friends after that. And she eventually joined that same church.

In July 1977, I started pounding the pavement to find an apartment. I didn't like being crammed into one bedroom with another baby coming soon. My uncle's wife was pleasant and took special care of Christine while I worked. Jeff had gotten laid off from the candy factory, but with the help of his dad, he landed a union job with the gas company delivering utility bills. In a couple of weeks, I found a two-bedroom apartment in a second floor duplex. The landlord was a sweet, elderly woman whose middle-aged son lived in the first floor apartment. The rent was $180 a month, and she promised to lower it once the new baby arrived. She kept her word, and we faithfully paid her every month's rent on time.

Our two-story duplex was a corner unit on a beautiful tree-lined street. The living room was at the front of the house, which was directly across the street from a large church. Now how cool was that? From our front window we could see the adjacent intersection and passing highway traffic. Next to the living room was the bathroom, a nice sized kitchen, the children's bedroom, and then our bedroom, which faced the back driveway. The hallway led to the stairs down to the first floor entry door, which opened into a shared foyer. It was perfect for us, and Jeff and I were thrilled. We sat on the hardwood floor and leaned against the wall of our empty living room. We giggled with excitement about having a place of our own and talked about how we would decorate it and entertain our family and friends. We talked about cooking our own meals for a change and finally sleeping in a room of our own that we didn't have to share with the baby. Our dreams took off, and our imaginations soared. Just before it was time for me to go on maternity leave, we purchased living room furniture, a TV, a dinette set, and we set up house. This was wedded bliss.

It was hot. I was tired, and I was very fat. I sat on the edge of the sticky chair in front of the fan that blew lukewarm air. Sweat poured from my face and neck and beneath my heavy breasts. I just couldn't cool off. I wiped my face with a damp cloth. The baby was three weeks past the due date, and I was scheduled to go to the hospital that morning to have labor induced. However, the hospital was busy and full with deliveries from the previous night. I was told to come back later.

We decided that it would be a good idea to walk the baby down and I accompanied Jeff on his rounds to deliver gas bills. All I had to do was stand on the corner of each block and keep an eye on the bag full of bills. He'd run up the street and pick up a bundle, deliver one side of the street, and then pick up another bundle and deliver the other side of the street. As I walked across each block, I began to appreciate what he was going through and what he was doing to provide for his family.

I knew he didn't like the job, but he did it for our growing family. Watching him run up and down the street caused me to understand that he would do anything to take care of us, and I loved him for it. I started to have contractions and told him that it was time to go to the hospital.

We arrived sometime late Thursday afternoon and continued with 18 grueling hours of labor. I begged for an epidural, just as I had with Christine's delivery, but it didn't seem to help. I eventually delivered a healthy eight pound, six ounce baby boy. Jeffery, Jr., joined our family at 7:14 a.m. on Friday, September 24, 1977, and he was simply beautiful. He had a head full of long, straight black hair that swept over his light complexion. He almost looked like he had Indian in his blood because of his "good" hair. He was the biggest baby and the only boy in the nursery during our stay. We were ecstatic and proud once again.

As I climbed the flight of stairs to our second floor apartment with a newborn and watched our one year old daughter walking about, I knew I had to get on some form of birth control. No matter how much Jeff would object, I just had to do something. No doubt about it.

***

Reflection:

Premarital counseling is essential for any couple considering marriage. Counseling would have raised red flags concerning power and control issues, and we might have learned what equality looks like in a marriage.

3
Let the Beatings Begin

"Dearly beloved, avenge not yourselves, but rather give place unto wrath: for it is written, Vengeance is mine; I will repay, saith the Lord." – Romans 12:19

"How much more grievous are the consequences of anger than the causes of it" – Marcus Aurelius

I was still on maternity leave when he got fired. He had not delivered gas bills one day and decided to double up on a subsequent day. When he told his supervisor about the change in plans, he was fired. Union intervention could not get his job back. He was depressed and sulked for hours at a time. He would leave the apartment early and stay out late. He wouldn't talk to me and stopped going to church altogether. At first I felt sorry for him and empathized with his feelings of worthlessness. But when he refused to talk to me, I became indifferent toward him.

Then one night I pressed him to talk and got something that I wasn't expecting. He confessed that he had cheated on me. I excused the transgression and forgave him quickly. We didn't have time to waste whining and pining over it. He was depressed, and I understood his pain of not being able to provide for his family. I had to offer him forgiveness, because God had forgiven me for my sins. How could I hold this one transgression against him? It was just a hiccup, and he must've felt horrible for sinning against God, as well.

His gratitude to me for forgiving him made me feel powerful and superior. I felt so invincible that I got up from the kitchen table, walked over to him, and let him cry in my arms. He seemed sincerely remorseful and apologized for hurting me. He begged me not to leave him. I felt as though I was his judge and jury and that, by forgiving him, I would indebt him forever to me. Surely, he would hold me in high esteem and respect me and wouldn't cheat on me again. That's what I thought. At least, that's what I was hoping for.

His repentant heart led him to go back to church and become active again. We signed up for classes at the Bible institute and never missed a session. The program required us to attend classes, participate in discussions, and pass exams. After successfully completing the course, we received certificates that made us eligible to work in ministry at the church. Jeff joined the choir, went to all-night prayer on Fridays, and helped out on the prayer chain phone lines once again. I was proud that I had contributed to this resurrected sense of purpose and renewed dedication. Even though he was out of work, at least he was doing something constructive with his free time. He started visiting his parents more frequently and often came home with bags of food that his mother gave us to help tide us over until his unemployment check arrived. I believed he became humbled and appreciative of what our families were doing to help us during that time.

He even made special preparations to take me out to a wonderful restaurant atop a skyscraper in the city. The surprise dinner also included a surprise gift. A beautiful replica of a diamond studded bracelet. I knew that they weren't all real diamonds, but it looked very expensive and made an impression. He took pictures of me at the restaurant, opening the gift and beaming with delight. His expression of love for me only confirmed his true contrition and his desire to be good.

Jeff's increased presence in his old neighborhood led him to witness to his childhood friend, Kenny, who became a born-again Christian under Jeff's guidance. The two started hanging out together and Kenny was spending a lot of time at our apartment. I first met Kenny at our neighborhood recreation center pool on a hot summer afternoon in 1975. I sat on the edge of the pool watching Jeff splash around. I hadn't noticed that Kenny had been watching me from the other end of the pool. He came and sat along side me on the edge. Just as he introduced himself, Jeff jumped out of the pool, demanded to know from Kenny what he was saying to me, and shoved him away. The two sparred and shoved each other like playful little kids learning how to box. I couldn't tell if they were playing around or really fighting. I got up off the edge, got my towel, and moved away to the other side of the pool. Evidently, Kenny didn't know I was Jeff's girlfriend.

That incident had been my only interaction with him. And now, three years later, he was in our apartment like some long lost brother, and Jeff beamed with excitement about having a hand in Kenny's salvation. I was happy that Jeff was happy.

The city buses were on strike, and we had not had a car since the last one broke down. I would walk to a coworker's home nearby and ride with him to and from work. On one occasion I needed a ride to pick up party supplies, and Jeff asked Kenny to drive me. My coworker dropped me off at the train station after work, and Kenny met me there and drove me around to the party supply store, the bakery, and the card shop. I was grateful for his help and told him so.

As we approached my street, he pulled up along the side street, pulled into a parking spot, and put the car in park. I asked him why he was stopping around the corner from the apartment. Without hesitation, he grabbed me and kissed me. I pushed him away and sat there in shock for a moment. I thought, "What are you doing? Are you crazy?" I was surprised and yet somewhat flattered. I was caught terribly off guard but knew I had to get my butt out of the situation.

I tried to process what had just happened. Without a word I got my bags, scurried out of the car, and ran around the corner to my apartment. My heart was racing. I couldn't slow it down. I flew up the stairs, and Jeff greeted me with a big hug. I clutched him tightly. He felt my pounding heart and asked what was wrong. I said that it was running up all those stairs that exhausted me. But I knew I couldn't keep that lie and that I would have to tell him what had happened with Kenny. I planned to tell him later that night after the children were asleep.

I was lying on my right side with my back to him as he spooned himself against me in our bed. I couldn't see his facial expression as I related the events of the afternoon. With one sweep of motion Jeff flipped me over onto my back and glared at me. I was puzzled. I searched his face for understanding and found none.

"What's wrong?" I asked. I told him exactly what happened. I didn't do anything wrong. I was honest with him and didn't want any secrets between us. And I was careful not to put our marriage at risk by kissing Kenny back or lingering with him in the car. I had proved to Jeff that I was faithful and wasn't going to cheat on him as he did on me. All of a sudden, he punched me square on the left side of my face. I was in a daze and actually saw stars twinkling around my head. I couldn't believe that I had just felt my jaw crack. I tried to gain composure and balance myself to sit up but I was knocked back down again with another blow to the face and then two hard pounding blows to my left side. The shock of his fist against my body left me breathless and wide-eyed. My little pink plastic hair rollers were flying everywhere. I began gasping for air and I rolled to one side. My face began to sting sharply, and as I tried to sit up and gain equilibrium, he pushed me back down on the bed and alternately punched me in my sides with his fists, first with the right and then with the left. I felt like a boxer's punching bag.

I screamed with pain. "Pleeeease, Jeff, stop!"

He wouldn't let me up. I yelled louder for him to stop but was careful not to wake the children or the neighbors with my screams. I tried to protect my face and head but had left my body exposed, so I rolled up into a ball. And then, just as suddenly as the barrage started, it stopped. He must've realized what he was doing. He was breathing heavily, and my cries were muffled as I buried my head into my pillow that was now saturated with sweat and tears. I couldn't move. I was afraid to move. I was afraid that any sudden movement would provoke another assault on my already bruised body and broken spirit. I just lied still so as not to arouse any suspicion of life or breath. I thought any shift in my body's position could end in death. He got up and went into the living room. I must've laid there wide-eyed for several minutes, tense and listening. I fell asleep from exhaustion.

It was early the next morning, and the sunlight trickled into the room. I could hardly open my eyes. I had to go to the bathroom and struggled to put my feet on the floor. My body ached all over. As I shuffled down the hall, I could see Jeff in the living room lying on the couch. I slid into the bathroom, locked the door, and looked in the mirror. My thin, short hair was matted and limp against my head. The sweat had reversed the perm some, and little nappy locks started to form around my crown and at my neck. I remembered that my hair rollers flew out as I was being pulverized the night before.

I barely recognized myself as I peered at the reflection. My entire face ached, and my eyes were like slits. My top and bottom eyelids were so swollen that my crusty, short eyelashes were hardly visible. The left side of my face and cheek were shiny, tight, and swollen as though I had a supersized jawbreaker in my mouth. I could hardly open my mouth. I ran warm water against a washcloth and put it against my eyes to moisten them enough to open them a little wider so I could investigate the damage to my skin. My whole head throbbed and ached. It was Friday, and I couldn't go to work looking like I did. I headed for the phone, dialed my coworker to say I wouldn't need a ride, called in sick, and went back to bed.

What Mommy said and Daddy did

A few hours later the phone rang. Jeff did not answer the nagging ring. It took me a long time to reach over the side of the bed to answer it. My side hurt badly, and I started to cry as I heard my mother's voice. She wanted to know why I wasn't at work. I told her about the beating. She was furious, and I heard her yell out to my father to come to see about me.

About an hour later or so the doorbell rang. It rang again and again. I struggled to get up out of bed. I slowly dragged myself down the stairs to let my father in, but by the time I got to the door, he was gone. I felt abandoned and insignificant. Why couldn't he wait? I was on my way to the door. It was at that moment that I realized that I was all alone. I couldn't depend on my father for help, and I had no one else to help me. I had to depend on myself. I slowly climbed up the stairs sniffling and whimpering, gripping my side with every step. Jeff was still in the living room. He hadn't budged.

My mom later told me that my dad left because he didn't want to lose his ride, since his friend didn't want to wait. After all, the city buses were on strike.

What my husband said

Jeff came into the bedroom and knelt beside the bed. He reached for me hesitantly at first and then with a gentle touch moaned out an apology. He told me that he didn't know why he reacted that way and was so very sorry for hurting me. He begged for my forgiveness again and asked what he could do to make it up to me. I asked him to let me rest. He obliged, but not before reaching for my hands and holding them between his as he prayed asking God for forgiveness. He prayed and cried a long time, and as I listened all I could think about was offering him the forgiveness that God had offered me.

After his heartfelt prayer, he got up and tended to the children. I stayed in bed the rest of the day.

What my coworker said

I went back to work on Monday. My coworker immediately noticed the swollen jaw and questioned me. I told her that Jeff and I were roughhousing over the weekend and that he accidentally hit me. She didn't believe me and said that he shouldn't be roughhousing around my face. I'll never forget that look of disgust on her face. She was quite indignant and rolled her eyes at me. I presumed that she was upset about him hitting me and even more upset with me for lying about it.

What my doctor said

By Thursday the following week, my side was hurting me so much that I walked to the neighborhood clinic. The doctor asked me about my face, and I told him the same thing I had told my coworker. I told him that I must've fallen on something and hurt my side while we were playing around, because it hurt every time I took a breath. They took x-rays, and the doctor told me that my ribs were badly bruised. He gave me a prescription for pain pills and a brace and told me to take it easy.

What my pastor said

I made an appointment to see the pastor. Surely he would give me direction on how to handle this delicate situation. He greeted me warmly as I entered the small meeting room just off the sanctuary on the side of the pulpit. I told him that my husband punched me in the face and that he bruised my ribs. I told him that Jeff said he was sorry.

He looked at me with compassion and said, "Well, what did you do to make him hit you?"

I wasn't expecting to hear that I was the cause of my misfortune. I frantically searched for an answer. "What did I do?" It never occurred to me that I could've caused the beating. The possible reasons engulfed me. Maybe I wasn't a good wife. Maybe I enticed Kenny without even knowing it. Maybe my dresses and skirts weren't long enough. Maybe I wore too much lipstick. I racked my brain trying to figure out what I had done wrong to invite such a pummeling. I left the meeting feeling that I was at fault and that I deserved to be hit. I resolved that I wasn't going to let anything like that happen again. I would not give my husband any reason to be suspicious of me. I was going to be a better wife.

The pastor told me that he would assign a deacon to mentor Jeff and admonished me not to provoke him. I accepted his advice but was deeply disappointed that he didn't offer any guidance on what I should do to protect myself. And I was disheartened that Jeff wasn't called on the carpet for hitting me.

What my girlfriend said

A few days later a girlfriend visited me. I didn't want to make time to sit, relax, and chat. I was too busy cleaning and scrubbing down the kitchen and making sure that everything was spotless and in its place. She asked what had happened to my face, and I told her about what happened and said that part of it was my fault. I said that I should not have gotten into a compromising situation with another man by being alone with him in his car. I encouraged her to be a faithful wife, and I boasted that I would never cheat on my husband or get into a situation like that again. I said that adultery was a sin and that God wanted us to be obedient to His Word. And then I quoted the Bible verse in Ephesians 5:22, "Wives, submit yourselves unto your own husbands, as unto the Lord";

and 1 Peter 3:1, "Likewise, ye wives, *be* in subjection to your own husbands; that, if any obey not the word, they also may without the word be won by the conversation of the wives." My young friend listened intently and seemed to soak up my advice and wisdom.

***

Jeff was angry with me about something and stayed out all night one night, and when I questioned him, he gave me that look -- the same look he gave me the night he nearly broke my jaw and the night he spit in my face. As he stood in the doorway of the kitchen, he stared at me without saying a word, and I knew something bad was about to happen. All of a sudden, he hurled the wooden hair brush he had been holding at me, and it hit my forehead hard. His aim was precise, and I was dazed for a moment. I instinctively raised my hand and put pressure on my head, and as my eyes began to water the throbbing pain began to overtake me. It took me a few more seconds to compose myself while he stood in the same spot in the doorway and watched me with fiery eyes. Then he walked away into another room. A few moments later, a shiny golf-ball sized lump appeared on the right side of my forehead. I cracked open a tray of ice cubes, wrapped them in a washcloth, and applied it to my head.

The next morning, I spent several minutes trying to comb and style my hair to hide the injury. I again wished to have hair like my sisters -- long, thick, and full. But, my hair wasn't long enough to form a bang to cover the lump, and no matter how hard I tried to sweep the fine, thin strands of mousy brown hair over my forehead, it just wouldn't do the trick. I thought maybe, just maybe, nobody would notice. I had to fix myself up in a hurry and get the kids ready. We were on our way to church, and I didn't want us to be late.

Our friends had invited us to their home for dinner after church that afternoon. Throughout the day, I kept combing my fingers through my hair trying to sweep it over the lump.

As I held my toddler son on one hip and mulled over the assortment of appetizers and entrée selections on the table, Jeff snapped our picture with a Polaroid camera. When the picture finally developed, I could see that I was tall, slim, and regal in my navy blue skirt and crisp white blouse. I had smooth, clear, dark brown skin with long hands and clean fingernails. I wore large brown-rimmed glasses, and then I saw it. A nice, shiny golf-ball-sized lump sat big and bold on my forehead. It glared at me like a big neon sign that read "my husband hit me in the head with a wooden hairbrush yesterday, and I couldn't cover it up." Jeff took other pictures and passed the developed photos around that afternoon. I eventually got the photo back and put it in my pocketbook. Nobody said anything about that photo or about that glaring neon sign.

Over the next several months, our frustrations with each other often led to arguments or some form of emotional or physical abuse. The deacon who was assigned to mentor Jeff tried to inspire him to live a consistent Christian life and attempted to become a friend. Jeff complained to me that the deacon was soft and too effeminate for him, so Jeff limited his interaction with him. There were times when Jeff was so depressed that I would call the deacon to come over just to get Jeff out of bed. I was at my wits' end. But I couldn't stop to baby him.

There were bills to be paid and children to be cared for. There was an opening in housekeeping at the state hospital where I worked. I asked around and was able to get Jeff the job. He worked the late shift for a few months but complained about the hours and later quit. I felt like it was my responsibility to work to provide health insurance benefits and to get a steady income for the family. I was beginning to resent Jeff. I got him the job. I thought that the least he could do was work it out until he found something else.

He came in early one morning after being out all night again. He hadn't called and my worry had turned into anger. I suspected that he was with some girl. He climbed up the stairs of our apartment with one of his brothers in tow who quietly slipped into the living room to wait for Jeff. He spoke just above a whisper and said good morning to me. With a faintly pleasant response I replied good morning back. Jeff came back to the bedroom. He was going back out with his brother and had come in only to get a change of clothes, and I didn't like it. I stood in my nightgown and demanded to know why he hadn't called and what he had done the night before. He told me to lower my voice, because he didn't want to wake the children and he didn't want his brother to hear us argue. I was so mad I kicked him in his shin with my bare foot.

He returned the favor and kicked me in both my shins. He was wearing steel-toed boots. As he was kicking me he emphasized each word in a measured beat and said, "Oh-so-you-want-to-kick-me-now. Well-how-does-this-feel?"

The pain ricocheted up one leg and down the other, and I grabbed the leg that had started to bleed. I flopped on the bed and winced. He yelled to his brother that he was ready to go, and out they went. I was still cradling and rubbing my legs as he slammed the door. I never kicked him again.

On another occasion, Jeff demanded that I write him a check for spending money when he went out. I told him that our checking account was low, that bills needed to be paid, and that we just couldn't afford it. We started to argue, and we were so loud that our downstairs neighbor heard us and called the cops. One of the police officers who responded to the call was our next door neighbor. I was embarrassed and, by this time, totally exhausted from arguing with Jeff. The officers told Jeff to leave and take a walk, but he said that he wasn't going anywhere unless I wrote the check. The banks were closed anyway, and since I wasn't physically injured and wanted him out of the house, I wrote the check to appease him.

After he left, I went to bed. He didn't come back home that night. The next morning, after taking the kids to a babysitter, I went straight to the bank and waited for it to open. I closed the checking account before Jeff could cash that check. He called me at work and sarcastically commended me for thwarting his plan. From that day forward, I never held a significant joint account with Jeff.

***

It must've been well after midnight when I heard muffled voices in my sleep, including a woman's voice. Startled, I jumped out of bed. I realized that I wasn't dreaming and that the woman's voice was real and was coming from my living room. I rushed to put on my thin housecoat and slippers. My heart pounded hard against my chest as I raced into the living room.

I couldn't believe my eyes. This man had the audacity to bring some woman into my home while I was there sleeping in my bed. He must be stupid and crazy, or I must be the dumbest person alive. He looked up startled as though he had expected me to sleep through her entire visit. Then he introduced me as if I were his sister or something. I didn't hear the reason for the visit, how the two had met, or how long ago they met. I couldn't hear anything more, because I was fuming inside. I had to think fast and not overact to give him more cause to act recklessly. But I was going to do something. I wasn't going to act like some deranged and jealous wife and make a big scene or start a fight. I was better than that. I had dignity and class.

As I composed myself and developed my plan of taking the high road, I politely asked our guest if she was hungry and if she wanted some of the bread pudding I had baked earlier that evening. She accepted the offer, and I led her into the kitchen. I watched her every move as she sat at my kitchen table and ate some of my bread pudding. I knew she felt my steely eyes upon her every gesture, word, and movement. She remarked to Jeff how sweet a person I was and then said how nice it was to meet me as she left. I don't remember what brought her to my living room that night, but I felt a sense of pride for controlling myself and not acting crazy. On second thought, I probably should've acted a fool and went ballistic on both of them. But instead, I went back to bed, and he slept on the couch.

***

During this period of unbecoming behavior, and one time in particular, Jeff, brought home something else with curves -- a bottle of vodka. The sight of the liquor bottle disturbed me. It reminded me of the awful fights my mother had with my father when he was drunk, and I didn't want to relive those traumatic events as an adult. The bottle sat on the kitchen counter, and one night, while Jeff was out I emptied the liquor out of the bottle and replaced it with water. I know it wasn't a smart thing to do, but I did what I felt was appropriate at the time. I wanted him to know that I simply could not tolerate liquor in my own home. The next day, he told me that if I ever did that again, he'd just buy a bigger bottle of vodka the next time. And I never did it again.

***

But, every now and then there would be a glimmer of hope for our relationship, and Jeff would show signs of optimism, bouncing back to sanity and his former cheerful self. I recommended that he see a doctor for what I suspected was depression and that we schedule an appointment to see a marriage counselor. I was sick and tired of his bouts of silence, which had become more frequent since he started to drink. He agreed that he needed help and wanted desperately to be back in full fellowship at the church.

He did go to the doctor, who prescribed some medication. Jeff complained that the medicine made his mouth dry and that it decreased his sex drive. I was glad about the decreased sex drive part, but I didn't want him to feel manipulated by me into taking drugs that would make him feel worse. The doctor prescribed something else, but again Jeff complained.

He didn't see an immediate effect and abruptly stopped taking the antidepressant.

On the first and last visit to a marriage counselor, I complained that Jeff was an alcoholic because he drank a beer every day. The Black male counselor told me that drinking a beer a day doesn't make you an alcoholic and that there was nothing wrong with that. I was insulted. I told him that I knew what an alcoholic was because my father was one. They both laughed at me. I understand now that equating drinking a beer-a-day to alcoholism was extreme, but at the time, I was suffering from what I had experienced as a child. I don't recall if we ever discussed why I was so afraid of alcohol, but I told Jeff that I wasn't going to that counselor again and that we needed to find a different one. We didn't go back. And we didn't find another counselor either.

Jeff made halfhearted attempts at appearing spiritual. Sometimes he'd go to church with us and sometimes not. The deacon continued to include Jeff in meetings with other young men at the church, and Jeff became friends with a few. He invited one young man, his new bride, and her two small children to live with us. Jeff had not asked my opinion or permission about it. I was annoyed, but I understood his compassion for this family. We were in their situation at one time in our lives as well. I wanted others to see that he was the head of our family, and I didn't want to embarrass him or usurp his authority by refusing to let them stay with us. However, I wished that he had discussed this with me before offering our home to people I barely knew.

Can you imagine two families living in a two-bedroom apartment? There were eight of us. It was cramped, but we made the best of it. Jeff worked temp jobs, and his friend, Tyrone, had a full-time job. His wife Sondra was pregnant, and she stayed at home with the children. It was nice to come home at the end of a long day and have another woman in the house to help with the cooking, cleaning, and child care. And it was especially nice to finally have someone to talk to.

Our families went to church services and Bible studies together. We were learning more and more about Christian marriage, and I was beginning to understand how the relationship between a man and his bride was to resemble God's relationship to the church, which was the body of believers. I learned that God so loved the world that He gave His Son for us. I learned that husbands ought to love their wives as their own body.

With all this new knowledge and seeing the newlyweds' love for each other in action, it helped to improve our marriage a little. I enjoyed seeing them so happy. I wanted that for us and tried desperately to latch on to anything that resembled happiness. I was a hopeless romantic and wanted people to know that somebody loved me. In spite of all my faults, somebody loved me.

I wanted to wear the symbol of eternal promise and love for the world to see, so I purchased my own diamond engagement ring. Jeff didn't think engagement rings were necessary and had never bought me one. We wore only gold bands with glass chips in them. But I longed to have an engagement ring and had asked him several times to buy me one. He never did. So I bought one for myself, and this time, it was a real diamond.

Finally, our adopted family found their own home and moved out. I was happy for them and relieved to get my space back, but I missed them, too.

Shortly after they left, Jeff left, too. He went to find work in Washington, DC, and lived with one of his sisters. He got a job at a new toy store chain and stayed for a few months into the Christmas season. I developed the routine of a single parent and didn't mind it so much. It was challenging for the first few weeks until Jeff got his first paycheck. But then he'd regularly send us money through Western Union. He would call and talk to the kids and ask how things were going. But he missed his family and eventually came home shortly after the New Year.

***

By the summer of 1981, I was getting restless working at the state psychiatric hospital and decided to look for another job. I got an interview at a major engineering and construction company in downtown Philadelphia for a job as secretary to the Vice President of Business Development. My interview strategy included outlining my credentials to Mr. Fred Carpenter and his boss and then phoning the next day. I vividly remember wearing a long-sleeved cream chiffon dress that flowed delicately in the summer breeze of that August afternoon. I had prayed that God would give me that job and was confident that my experience and skills would help, too.

In the post-interview phone call, I thanked Mr. Carpenter for the interview and explained that there were two purposes for my call. One was to let him know that I was very interested in the job, and the other was to give him the opportunity to hear my telephone voice so he'd know how I would come across to his clients and potential clients. That phone call cinched it, and I was hired.

Fred had relocated from Boston. I assisted him in the transition by setting up his new office and filing system. He was married with three children. He was about six feet tall with dark hair and quite attractive for a middle-aged man. While working together, I learned quite a bit about how to handle difficult people and developed some sales strategies, as well as how to assert myself professionally. The company was on the cutting edge of technology and our sales department was one of the first departments to use the new word processing equipment. I worked with the pilot word processing team in preparing proposals. I delivered them to local prospective clients, set up hospitality suites at industry conferences, trained and supervised other secretaries in the department, and enjoyed lavish lunches, dinners, and after-work functions.

Fred spared no expense when we had meals together and never missed a reason to celebrate special days like secretary's day or my birthday. He showed his appreciation for my work, and I provided top-notch secretarial support for him. I even took trips to New York City and Denver to personally deliver proposals. With each of these trips I enjoyed a heighted sense of freedom and confidence. I felt alive and mentally stimulated whenever I embarked on an assignment outside my routine. I was intoxicated by it. Jeff sensed this intoxication and knew he couldn't compete. He knew I loved my job and enjoyed working with Fred. Fred challenged me to stretch my limits and do things out of the norm. Jeff was jealous that my attention to my job overshadowed him. Jeff tried hard to sober me up and bring me back to his reality.

Since Jeff couldn't curb my enthusiasm about my job, he decided to join me. I suspect that he just wanted to keep an eye on me. Within a year, I was able to get Jeff a job at the engineering firm where I worked. He worked in the drafting department on another floor, and I rarely saw him during the day. And that's the way I liked it. I didn't like the idea of working with my husband in case our home life interfered with our work life. I was definitely opposed to the idea and kept a good distance from his work area. I didn't even want anyone to know we were married.

I had developed a great deal of self-confidence and was dressing more professionally than I had in my other job. We now had two incomes, and some sense of stability had settled in. It didn't last long before Jeff started acting up again.

***

Jeff was scurrying around the apartment trying to get ready, ironing his shirt, and asking me where the shoe polish was. He was asked to be a model at some fashion show event, and I asked if I could go along with him. He told me I couldn't and that I needed to stay with the kids. I said that I could get a sitter and still go, but he rejected my idea. That's when I suspected that another woman was involved somewhere in this picture. Here we go again. He took the car and left.

I wasn't going to stay cooped up in the apartment all day, so I dressed the kids and we went to visit Jeff's parent's home where his sister and brother were living. It was a nice day, and late that afternoon Jeff showed up. But he didn't come alone. You guessed it -- he was with another woman.

His sister's boyfriend was outside sitting on the steps as Jeff approached the house, and he warned Jeff that I was inside. Jeff didn't care and boldly proceeded up the steps into the house with the woman trailing behind. He started introducing the woman to everyone, and when he got to me, I interrupted and said that I was his wife. Jeff had been drinking. As I declared my affiliation with Jeff, I announced to everyone, while looking directly at the woman, that Jeff wasn't wearing his wedding ring and that Jeff had misled her. He remarked that I would notice something as trivial as that. I was humiliated. I told Jeff to take me home. He said that he couldn't and that he'd be home after he dropped her off. I gathered the kids and asked Jeff's brother and his girlfriend to take us home.

The next morning was Sunday and I wasn't in the mood to go to church. Jeff hadn't come home that night, and I was still suffering from being disgraced the day before. My girlfriend called and tried to comfort me and convince me to go to church, but I said no and told her that I would just stay home. Instead, I called Jeff's brother and his girlfriend and asked them to pick up the kids for me for the day. I needed a break. When Jeff finally got home later that afternoon I told him that our marriage was in trouble and that it was over. He pleaded with me to forgive him. He kissed me hard and passionately and I remembered how much I had loved him. He squeezed me tightly. I didn't resist and melted in his arms. I thought, "He really does love me even though he's stupid when he's drunk."

But those feelings were short-lived. We stayed up late that night and Jeff began to confess to all the wrong he had done. He told me how he would take the children to the babysitter and bring other women to our apartment while I was at work. He told me how easy it was for him to pick up these women just by walking down the street and about how he unintentionally brought one of them back to our bed. Normally, he'd use the couch. I was mortified.

By the next morning, I felt worthless and stripped of all sense of dignity. Not only was I presented with the truth and realized that the man I loved was depraved, I was forced to do something about it. How could he be a Christian and act like the devil? Didn't he believe anything he had learned about God and marriage? There seemed to be no hope for us, and I just couldn't wrap my brain around what he had done.

I called my mother, packed up my kids and our clothes, and left.

***

Reflections:

1. Domestic abuse is a marriage deal-breaker. The cycle of domestic abuse I experienced involved (i) abuse; (ii) guilt; (iii) honeymoon or normal period; (iv) tension building and set up; and then back to (v) a violent incident.

2. Adultery is a marriage deal-breaker. Some marriages can survive adultery if both parties have intense therapy and counseling.

3. I struggled with the idea of retaliating, since the Biblical principles of an eye-for-an-eye and turning the other cheek are conflicting concepts. However, there are several comforting Bible Scriptures that deterred me from plotting revenge, such as:

    a. Deuteronomy 32:35 which says, "To me *belongeth* vengeance, and recompence; their foot shall slide in *due* time: for the day of their calamity *is* at hand, and the things that shall come upon them make haste."

b. Psalm 140:4 "Keep me, O Lord, from the hands of the wicked; preserve me from the violent man; who have purposed to overthrow my goings."

4
Reconciliation

*"The Lord will give strength unto his people;
the Lord will bless his people with peace." – Psalm 29:11*

*"When we long for life without difficulties, remind us that
oaks grow strong in contrary winds and diamonds are made
under pressure." – Peter Marshall*

Jeff kept calling my mom's house apologizing and pleading for me to forgive him and come back. I told him that I would not go back to the apartment and would not consider accepting him back unless two conditions were met. I said that I wanted him to recommit himself fully to the Lord and to find our family a home. I was going to get what I wanted this time. He promised to do whatever it took to get his family back and said that he wanted to move out of Philly and away from the bad influences. He thanked me for giving him another chance and apologized for messing things up so badly. He was now on his way to making me happy.

I had to work late on a proposal, and he was supposed to pick me up from work. I waited and waited outside the building until I finally gave up and took the bus. When I got off the bus and turned the corner of my mother's street, I noticed our parked car.

I picked up my pace and stormed through the front door into the house. My adrenalin level was high, and I was not amused as I watched him sitting at the kitchen table laughing, playing cards, and drinking beer with a couple of his buddies. I began screaming and yelling at him demanding to know why he hadn't picked me up. I wasn't thinking about how crazy I must've looked as I went back into the dining room looking for something to throw at him.

I picked up one of the pieces of plastic fruit that sat in a glass bowl as the centerpiece of the table and threw it at him. I picked up another and then another, yelling and screaming and throwing until the bowl was empty. He blocked each thrown piece and laughed at my hysteria. Come to think of it now, I really did overreact. But it seemed like a good release of pent-up anger at the time, and the situation was way over my tolerance level. The brightly-colored hollowed out plastic shapes of apples, oranges, and bananas were scattered on the floor between the kitchen and dining room.

Jeff had stopped laughing by the time I was through and was now heading toward me. My mother had heard all the commotion from upstairs and raced down. I'm sure our neighbors heard the noise as well. I did not realize that I had left the front door open on my way in. Jeff's friends couldn't catch him before he grabbed a hold of me. I was prepared to punch him as hard as I could, but my mother and his friends separated us. Jeff left the house with his friends in-tow and drove off.

I was exhausted, sweaty, and hot. I regained some form of composure and went to the front door to get some air. My neighbor and childhood friend, Scott, had heard the clatter and was standing in the doorway of his house across the street with his German shepherd at his side. They both looked over at me. Scott didn't say a word. He just looked at me and then he looked up and down the street. He was a couple of years older than me, and I considered him my big brother. I sat down on the steps and sniffled. As I closed my eyes and let the wind whip across my sweaty face, I took a deep breath. I felt safe. I knew that Scott would stand there as long as I needed him to.

I felt like he was standing guard over me, and I knew that he would fight for me and protect me if I needed him. He stood outside for a long time after I went back into the house. He would be ready in case Jeff came back. But Jeff did not come back that night.

***

One Saturday morning, I was sorting the dirty clothes into three piles on the bedroom floor – whites, light-colored, and dark-colored. I was going to the local Laundromat because my mom's washing machine wasn't working. The kids were downstairs watching TV. My mom came into the room to tell me that she had heard some things about Jeff that I should know. She said that he was seen drinking with women in a local bar. I wondered how she could know that since she didn't hang out with his circle of friends. She didn't know what she was talking about, I thought. I told her that I wasn't interested in hearing any gossip. I knew that she did not like Jeff, so I thought she was just passing gossip to rile me up. I thought she was trying to give me ammunition so I would divorce him, after which she could declare that he was no good and say she told me so.

I didn't want to live with my mother any longer than I needed to, and there was no way she was going to stop me from reaching my goal. We were going to buy the house that Jeff had found for us and would move out within a few weeks. All I needed to do was to stay focused.

A few weeks before, we found out that one of our coworkers was being transferred and needed to sell his house right away. Jeff was interested in buying it and had inquired about seeing the property. I was excited and thankful that the Lord heard my prayers. We took the 30-minute drive to a lovely tree-lined main street on the edge of town that had townhouses on one side and the Widener College campus on the other. The elementary school, park, playground, and college track and field were only one block away. The two-story, three-bedroom house was situated in the middle of the block just at the crest of the hill and there was a large rhododendron bush on the front lawn that made it stand out.

It was a warm summer evening, and the light breeze was just perfect for that time of year. There were two sets of steps separated by a landing that led to the front door. As I approached the top step and opened the screen door, I pressed my hand along the door frame and prayed a simple prayer of faith aloud, "I claim this house as mine in the name of Jesus." Our offer was accepted that very evening.

The mortgage application process took about two months, and I was surprised that we qualified so easily. The house cost $36,000, with an 11% fixed rate for 30 years. Our credit was pretty good, and we were able to get FHA financing. We had reached our goal. At 27 years of age, I owned my own home -- something my mother and father had not achieved -- and I felt truly fortunate to be a homeowner. I knew I made them proud, and even though Jeff and I had our share of marital problems, it didn't stop us from setting and achieving goals for our family. We believed that we could accomplish just about anything if we worked together as a team; and as long as we had the Lord on our side and remained obedient to His commandments, things would work out. We moved in on October 30, 1983.

***

During a routine gynecology exam that following spring, the doctor could not locate my intrauterine device and scheduled a D&C to find and replace it. On the day of the procedure, tests revealed that I was pregnant and that it was an ectopic pregnancy. The routine procedure had turned into a surgical one. I was overwhelmed by getting the news of being pregnant, then having surgery, and then not being pregnant all in the same day. But I began to thank God when I realized that I could've collapsed in the street somewhere with a ruptured fallopian tube and been rushed to the hospital for emergency surgery. That would've been frightening.

A tear trickled down the side of my face as I lay there in the hospital bed. Jeff was with me the whole time and was a great comfort. He hovered over my every move, held my hand, wiped my tears, and prayed for me. We both knew that, because I was anemic, complications could arise, and I could possibly require a transfusion if I lost a lot of blood. But the surgery went well, and a blood transfusion wasn't necessary. However, I did have a long recovery period to build up my strength and blood count before returning to work.

During the following weeks, while I was busy with the kids, working, and keeping house, Jeff would visit neighborhood churches on the weekends to find our family a place to worship. We were determined to leave Philly behind us and start fresh in this new town. He had met a man in his travels about town who told him about a small group that met weekly for Bible study in someone's home just around the corner from us. Jeff decided to take us there one Wednesday night.

After visiting a couple of times, Jeff decided that we would join this small Bible study group. Pretty soon the leaders, Alvin and Maxine Motley, invited us to become part of the larger group that gathered on Sundays at the Lighthouse Church in the next town. The Lighthouse Church became our home church, and we were received with open arms. The Mennonite congregation, at about two hundred members, was a lot smaller than the Pentecostal church we left behind, which had over three thousand. It was more intimate and offered a true sense of family and belonging. I was pleased with his decision.

Jeff became very involved in the church ministry and was later appointed deacon. However, he really didn't like the appointment. He thought it was beneath him and believed that he had a higher calling. He wanted to serve as an evangelist, and over the years, people had prophesied that he would be a leader in the church or a preacher. He had the gift of gab and could persuade anyone to his way of thinking. A deacon was a servant, not a leader. A deacon's role was to visit the sick and handicapped and to do whatever routine tasks that the pastor needed, such as daily maintenance and housekeeping of the church building. Even though Jeff wasn't thrilled with his assignment, he acquiesced and obediently performed the tasks.

Not long after that, Jeff was leading street-witnessing teams in Chester's inner city, preaching, teaching, giving out tracts, and telling others about Jesus. He'd load up the van with tables, chairs, Bibles, and the portable sound system. He would assign other Church members their tasks, set up the sound system and, with the microphone in hand, compel bystanders and passers-by to accept Jesus as their Lord and Savior. People stopped and listened. Some even got saved.

Jeff faithfully attended men's fellowship meetings and Sunday school classes and was asked to speak at several special events around town. As a couple, we worked with the evangelism ministry, in the children's ministry, and in the nursery, and we occasionally led Bible study classes. We were assigned kitchen and fellowship hall duties and greeter duty on Sunday mornings on a rotating basis with other families. Our children made friends, and finally Jeff had a group of Christian men he could talk to. I was glad that he had friends he could confide in and work with. I enjoyed seeing my family so content and emotionally healthy. Finally.

We opened up our home and began hosting dinner parties and meetings, and Jeff became a well-respected leader in the church and in the community. We celebrated our tenth wedding anniversary with a few of our closest friends and family at a Japanese Hibachi style restaurant in Ole' City Philadelphia. This sense of belonging and accomplishment felt good. I didn't want it to end.

Over the next few years, our lives settled into a routine. I got another job in 1985 in the human resources department of a chemical company. Our offices eventually moved from the city to a quiet suburb near my home. That cut down on my commuting time. Jeff got laid off from the engineering firm, and I got him a job in the mailroom with the chemical company. We'd go to work together, and I remember once sneaking kisses in the hallway before going our separate ways in the building, not realizing that we had been caught on the video surveillance camera. The security guards teased us endlessly about our outward expressions of affection. Our coworkers and new church family simply adored us and thought we were the perfect couple.

5
Five Deadly A's

"If you're going through hell, keep going."
– Winston Churchill

"Yea, though I walk through the valley of the shadow of death, I will fear no evil: for thou art with me; thy rod and thy staff they comfort me." – Psalm 23:4

In early 1989, we decided to have another baby, and I got pregnant right away. Jeff complained about working for someone else and wanted to start his own business, so we took out a loan and purchased an office cleaning franchise. The business required him to work evenings and sometimes into the night. He'd occasionally take the kids to help, and sometimes he'd go alone. Whenever he went alone, he wouldn't get home until the wee hours of the morning. He hired a small crew to help out with some of the larger accounts, and whenever someone called out or didn't show up, he'd have to juggle schedules. But he enjoyed being his own boss calling the shots. He was an excellent manager who demanded perfection and precision and would not tolerate laziness in his workers.

Things were running relatively smoothly, when out of the clear blue sky a storm came along that rocked my small world.

Early one morning on my way to work in the fifth or sixth month of my pregnancy, I got into the car and noticed a crumpled piece of paper under the armrest. Jeff had worked late and didn't get home until the wee hours of the morning with our car. We only had one car since the Volkswagen seized up on the expressway and was left abandoned a few weeks earlier. I read the crumpled hotel receipt in utter disbelief and became enraged. I thought that maybe I was just overreacting. Maybe the increased hormone levels due to the pregnancy caused me to be more suspicious and more emotional than normal.

The piece of paper was a hotel receipt for a night during which I assumed Jeff had worked. I planned to investigate it further when I got to work, but I was running late and could not go back into the house to confront him. By the time I got to work, I was so angry that I blasted Jeff on the phone and accused him of being with another woman. He brushed off my accusations and said that he had gotten the room because it was too late to come home and he was tired. He told me I was exaggerating. I couldn't take any more time at work screaming into the phone, so I hung up on him. I didn't want to believe my own gut instincts and talked to a coworker. I asked her if I was overreacting and if I needed to correct my thinking. She assured me that I had every right to be upset. She called the hotel and verified that there were two occupants in the room that night and that my suspicions were justified. I decided to do more investigative work and reviewed our home phone bills.

I had the phone bills and hotel receipt to prove that Jeff was indeed having an affair. However, I believed that it was my fault that he strayed. I tried to think of ways that I had contributed to such behavior but could not come up with anything. Our intimacy levels hadn't decreased even with my pregnancy. I thought we were content with our lives at this stage. I called our friend, Pastor Al, and asked him to talk to Jeff. I talked to my friend, Linette, and shared with her what was going on. She encouraged me to pray for Jeff and to take care of myself and the baby. She reminded me that I wasn't the problem and that Jeff had had issues for a long time. She prayed for my strength during the ordeal and reminded me that the Lord loved me just as I was.

In the meantime, my energy was spent cleaning the house in places that I had not seen in years. I vigorously moved furniture, vacuumed carpets and rugs, and mopped the floors over and over until they were squeaky clean and spotless. I scrubbed the bathroom, the kitchen, the walls, and the baseboards throughout the entire house. And then I recalled that every Saturday morning when I was a child, my mother made us do the same kind of cleaning ritual no matter how much we complained. I was turning into my mother and was afraid.

When I finally confronted Jeff about this unfaithfulness, he did not deny it. When I asked him about the details of the tryst, he obliged me, but he couldn't tell me why he did it. He asked for my forgiveness. And, again, I gave it. Again, I insisted that we go to marriage counseling and establish a system for him to be accountable to me and to someone else about his whereabouts. He accepted the conditions; and to prove to me that he was sincere about not cheating on me again, he went out and bought me a new car -- a navy blue 1989 Oldsmobile Ninety-Eight. This was the beginning of yet another honeymoon cycle.

Over the next few weeks, Jeff treated me like a queen. Our pastor nominated us to attend a couples' weekend retreat held at an upscale resort hotel sponsored by American Family Services, and we accepted the invitation. We thought this would be a great way to celebrate our 14th wedding anniversary. We attended group workshops on marriage, self revelation, forgiveness, and acceptance in addition to making private and public commitments to each other to work on our marriages. Each couple was encouraged to pray for one another and to write letters to their spouses expressing love and asking for forgiveness of past injuries. This is when I found out that at one point in our marriage Jeff had stopped feeling any love for me.

He said that he prayed over and over to God asking Him to give him love for me. Jeff told me that he was glad when God finally answered his prayers. But, I wasn't so sure that God had answered Jeff's prayers, because Jeff treated me so poorly.

We argued on the way home after the retreat, and it escalated once we walked in the door. So much for celebrating our anniversary. He had me pinned on the bed, and his hands were locked firmly around my neck. As I gasped for air I stopped seeing his face altogether. Instead, I saw flashes of past experiences of my life. The flashing scenes occurred in rapid succession like lightning bolts, and I could actually feel the emotion of each of the random events that I cannot recall now. I didn't feel any pain. I didn't feel myself gasping for air anymore. I felt like I was floating overhead looking down as if I were watching a scene from a movie. I later learned that what occurred to me was an out-of-body experience.

Then all of a sudden I was jolted back to reality. Jeff was shaking me and calling my name. It was as if I had been awakened from a deep sleep. I started to cough and opened my eyes. He wrapped his arms around me and began rocking me back and forth, moaning and sobbing. I mean, he was really crying hard. Then he started kissing me and apologizing for what he had done. I didn't feel any anger. I wasn't freaked out about being strangled almost to death. I was just intrigued about what I had experienced. Being so close to death and the transition into another realm had not frightened me at all. I felt confident in knowing that, if I did die, the Lord would be waiting for me on the other side. Jeff got down on his knees by the side of the bed and, while still crying, asked me to forgive him. He started praying and asked God to forgive him. I was seven months pregnant.

A month later, a snow storm hit. It was on the first Friday in December, and at my job employees were allowed to leave work early. It was stressful cleaning off my new car, driving a coworker home, and navigating in snowy weather on hilly narrow roads.

It took a long time to get home, and I was exhausted. Two days later on Sunday evening, I went into premature labor and was told to go to the hospital. My doctor ordered medication to stop the contractions, and after an overnight stay, he put me on complete bed rest for the remainder of my pregnancy. I had to start my maternity leave of absence early. Jeff took good care of me and the family during this time. He did all the cooking, cleaning, and household chores, in addition to managing his business. Two months went by quickly, and I went into labor just one day past the original due date. The contractions were extremely intense on the morning I delivered, and we arrived at the hospital at 1:30 in the afternoon. And just in time, too. Michelle Lynn was born an hour later at 2:36 p.m. on January 26, 1990. And she was simply beautiful.

Christine and Jeff, Jr. were happy to have a little sister and smothered her with affection and attention from the first day she was born. The wonder of God's creation in my arms overwhelmed me, and I would just sit and stare at her for long periods of time. It was not an inconvenience to get up in the middle of the night to feed her, to change her diaper, or to soothe her if she was afraid. I believe that I nurtured Michelle more than I had nurtured Christine and Jeff, Jr., and I regretted that. My being an older mother and having premature labor intensified my bond with her.

***

That tax season was especially stressful for us. Jeff insisted that I complete our income taxes every year, and this year it was difficult trying to separate his business expenses from his personal expenses. Whenever I questioned him about entries in the business checkbook, he got agitated. One night, I was cradling our two-month old baby while trying to decipher and categorize the receipts and balance his business checking account when I realized some money was unaccounted for. I got up from the dining room table and walked towards the living room while holding the baby and asked him to explain the discrepancy. He told me to make something up.

By this time, I was really frustrated. I thought that not only did I have to do the taxes for his sole proprietorship, but I had to also finagle numbers. I didn't like the fact that he was telling me to lie, and I started to manifest the irritation in my body language and attitude. I asked him again, but this time with an edge in my voice. He got up off the couch, rushed over toward me, and punched me hard in my stomach while I was holding Michelle. The blow slammed me against the dining room wall and down to the floor, but I didn't lose my grip on the baby. She started to cry as I struggled to catch my breath and regain composure. He stood over us and looked down.

I remained slumped on the floor up against the wall for a moment trying to comprehend what had just happened. This man hit me while I was holding our child. What a low-down, dirty dog, I thought. I just couldn't believe it. I managed to get up as he walked out of the room. He sat at the dining room table and sulked. I thought maybe he was just as bewildered as I was. I went upstairs, and he appeared shortly after trying to find words that could excuse the assault. The only words he could find were "I'm sorry, Lynn." I ignored his lame attempt at an apology. Over the next few days, I finished the taxes and never brought up the subject of his hitting me while holding our daughter. He knew he was wrong. I could see the guilt all over him. I promised myself that, one day, I would never do incomes taxes again. One day.

After all these years, I now knew how to play the game of guilt and how to manipulate Jeff. Whenever he felt bad about doing something wrong against me, I would be prepared to take advantage of the situation. But, unfortunately, I always bargained only for what was rightfully mine in the first place. I told him that I wouldn't deal with his business records anymore. It caused a lot of tension between us, and I told him to do the work himself, as well as take on the responsibility of paying all the household bills. I told him that I would concentrate on taking care of our children, maintaining the house, and volunteering as the church secretary. He agreed, and I was relieved.

We busied ourselves with family life, church work, and the cleaning business, and once again we were back on track. I extended my leave of absence for a year and enjoyed staying at home with the children and helping out at church. I assumed a few more administrative responsibilities at church and felt as though I had found my niche.

We celebrated our 15th wedding anniversary that November 1990 by inviting twenty couples to come along with us on a dinner cruise up the Delaware River. We dressed up in our finest and even videotaped the event. It was nice to have our family and friends with us.

Over the next year, Jeff tried his hand at politics and was asked to be the campaign manager for a woman running for mayor. She won by a landslide. Jeff was instrumental in her success and made a lot of friends along the way. His looks and his charisma drew many people to him, especially the women. By this time, I had returned to work. He acted as Mr. Mom and took Michelle with him everywhere. One time, when our family was invited to a picnic given by the Mayor at a local park, I was surprised to see unfamiliar women laughing and playing with my toddler and chumming up to Jeff. I felt a little uneasy, but quelled my suspicions and introduced myself to them. The women were part of the Mayor's staff, and I eventually became friends with a few of them.

Jeff's popularity increased and people gravitated to him. When one of the Mayor's staff asked Jeff to drive her to an appointment because she didn't have a car, I remembered my encounter years ago and the devastating effect it had on me, and I volunteered to take Jeff's friend to her appointment. There were other times when women in the church and in the community thought it was okay to ask Jeff to do things for them, but I cautioned Jeff about these seemingly innocent requests, and he delegated the requests to others.

A local minister asked Jeff to become involved in the evangelism ministry and community outreach program in his church. He also asked Jeff to lead Bible study at a local community center in Delaware. Jeff was given complete autonomy and directed the program from start to finish. This led to the formation of a new church that Jeff called Set Free Christian Fellowship. This new responsibility required our family to go out on Wednesday nights and early Sunday mornings into the projects in Wilmington.

The people were hungry for the Word of God, and a faithful few attended every meeting. Jeff, Jr., would help his father set up and operate the sound system. I led praise and worship with pre-selected songs that I prepared on overhead slides, and Christine would operate the projector. Sometimes our teenagers would protest or show lack of interest, but their father would enthusiastically coax them back into the program.

Our families were very supportive of Jeff's achievements and visited our small church when he made his pastoral debut. Around this time my youngest sister asked us to take in her seven year old son, Eric, who had some behavior issues. He was constantly fighting in school and being mischievous, and my sister believed that we could help him. We accepted Eric into our home, and during the next year his presence would affect our lives in a way that we could not have imagined.

***

Jeff asked me to preach a sermon on Mother's Day. I was honored and excited about sharing God's Word. I had become accustomed to leading praise and worship at church and wasn't shy about standing in front of people. For my job, I had conducted new hire orientations, given presentations, and lectured in front of small groups. I served as the company's tour coordinator and guide and was a member of the speaker's bureau leading presentations about recycling at local elementary and junior high schools.

I began the sermon with a joke about how God created Adam first and, realizing that He could do better than that, went on to create Eve. I spoke about the importance of a mother in the family and her rightful place alongside, and not behind, the husband in raising a family. I presented Bible Scriptures that exalted women and mothers, and I encouraged those listening to cherish the mothers in their lives. The message was well received, and it brought my husband to his feet with accolades and a lot of "Amens" from the congregation.

It didn't bother me that Jeff never asked me to preach again. I wasn't ordained as an evangelist or a pastor and was quite content being my husband's helpmate. I was not in competition with him. My role as a pastor's wife was simple. My assignment was to encourage him, to raise our children, and to keep his home a sanctuary from the stresses of ministry and work. But in my case, it also included working a full-time job outside of the home, helping to pay the bills, and helping him manage his business and the church business. Who was going to support me? Who was going to encourage me? Perhaps my assignment was not so simple after all.

The pressures of running a church and operating a business eventually took their toll on Jeff -- and on me. Our already overwhelming schedule took on an additional burden when Jeff agreed to another minister's request to merge his congregation with ours. When the members from the other congregation began to challenge Jeff's authority as pastor, things got ugly. One member had been entrusted to make bank deposits of the Sunday offerings on Jeff's behalf. It was discovered that she had been siphoning funds from the church's account. And when Jeff confronted her, she lied, so the woman was called on the carpet and relieved of her duties. Jeff was used to giving orders and wasn't accustomed to being challenged or lied to. Dealing with uncooperative people about important issues was wearing him thin, and he had no patience or tolerance for laziness or dishonesty. The deception and dissention discouraged him deeply.

He became depressed, sullen, and quiet. I encouraged him to talk to Bishop Jones, who had originally assigned him to this ministry. But Jeff would not reach out to the Bishop. Instead, he started staying out a little longer than usual. I didn't smell alcohol on his breath whenever he returned home, so I assumed he was just driving around to clear his head and to get away from it all. Little did I know that there was another adversary that I would have to deal with, another boulder to move. And the adversary had a name. Her name was Crack. Miss Crack Cocaine.

***

Reflections:

These five deadly A's were major deal-breakers in my marriage:

1. Abortion: I could not forgive myself for having an abortion. The silence and guilt crippled me, and I believed that I deserved all the misfortune I experienced in my life because of the horrible thing I did.

2. Abuse: Witnessing abuse of a parent is a high risk factor in being in an abusive relationship as an adult. I believed that fighting and conflict were acceptable or at least tolerable behaviors in a marriage.

3. Addiction: Family members can become enablers and perpetuate the addiction of a loved one.

4. Adultery: The humiliation of adultery and betrayal causes tremendous pain. Total healing and forgiveness are difficult to achieve.

5. Alcohol: As an adult child of an alcoholic, I could have become one of two extremes – either totally averse to any form of alcoholic beverages or an alcoholic myself.

PART II
THE BREAK DOWN

6
Wearing the Mask

*"He that covereth his sins shall not prosper: but whoso con-
fesseth and forsaketh them shall have mercy."*
– Proverbs 28:13

We were settling in for the night one Sunday evening after church and decided to watch a movie and eat popcorn. Jeff volunteered to go out and get some. He didn't come back home that night -- or the next. He was gone for four days. Finally, he called me at work Thursday morning to say that he was home and that he was tired. He apologized for not letting me know earlier that he was okay. When I got home from work that evening, he had already showered and was sulking in the bedroom away from everybody. He wouldn't talk to me about where he had been or what he had been doing. I was seething, but I understood that he probably needed some time to decompress from his escapade and regain his momentum. So, I didn't press him. I thought I had learned when not to approach the brooding lion.

It wasn't until Friday night when things got ugly. He had been in bed all day. A little after eleven o'clock, I finally got into bed. I snatched the covers and slammed my head against the pillow with my back to him. He knew that I was angry. I lay there with my eyes wide open. Be a man, Jeff, I thought. Confess your faults, ask forgiveness, and move on the way you normally do. Let's get past this mess. I was overwrought and wanted some answers. He could feel my agitation. I couldn't stand the silent treatment any more.

I turned over, facing his back leaning on my elbow, and in an irritated tone asked, "Well, where were you, Jeffery?"

I was harsh when I demanded to know where he had been for those long four days.

He didn't answer me. I slapped him against the back of his head insisting that he answer me or at least acknowledge that I was talking to him. My breathing was heavy, and I began to sweat not knowing what he would say. I didn't slap him hard. It was the kind of slap you'd give a child to get his attention if he were doing something mischievous and thought no one else was looking. It was the kind of slap that didn't cause pain or injury. It was just a snap-out-of-it kind of slap. I could feel my heart racing and my eyes getting even wider. What was his explanation? Was he having another affair? Where did he eat? Where did he wash? I knew he hadn't packed a bag, so he must've worn the same smelly, stinky clothes and skid-marked underwear for four days! The nasty, low-down dirty dog, I thought. I was angry and, by this time, very unreasonable. I was so mad I could spit fire. Here I am going to work every doggone day while he sits around doing nothing.

Then I had second thoughts. He must feel miserable to have cheated on me and to have deserted the family again. I wondered how could he face a congregation and preach the gospel of Christ knowing that during the past week he had been in some other woman's bed, eating her food, and watching her TV. He must feel awful. He must feel like a real hypocrite, and here I am insisting on knowing all the details of his betrayal. How could I judge him? How could I demand anything from him? After all, he was under a lot of pressure. Only God knows Jeff's heart, his frame of mind, and what he was really doing.

My mind was going haywire just thinking about what had happened to him during those four days. God forgive me for letting my imagination get the better of me. I almost felt sorry for him -- almost. He turned his whole body around to face me, and while leveraging himself with his left arm, he rose up over me and glared at me. I backed down and rested my head on the pillow. I recognized the look in his eyes. I had seen that icy stare many times just before all hell broke loose.

His facial expression told me that I was about to get a good beat down. As soon as I realized that I was about to be pummeled, I raised my hands and arms to cover my face, and he punched me hard. He punched me so hard in my left side that I howled as if I had been hit with a battering ram, the kind you see medieval armies use in the movies to crush a castle's gates. The powerful blow pushed me back, and my body involuntarily bounced forward off of his left arm. With one motion of the forward jerk, I jumped out of the bed to get away and flung myself to the floor against the wall, grabbing my side and writhing in pain.

I was trying to crawl away but couldn't catch my breath, and I couldn't move one inch farther. I gasped for air but couldn't catch it. When he had punched me in the jaw years ago, I saw stars, but this time I was in a daze so blinding that I couldn't see stars or react in any way. My body would not respond to what my brain wanted it to do. I was dizzy and needed the wall to help me determine which way was up. Just let me catch my breath, please God, just let me catch my breath, I thought. Once I was able to get air, I realized that Jeff had not lunged after me. He had not moved.

He was cradling his forearm and rocking back and forth on the bed. Realizing that he wasn't coming after me, I crawled on the floor around the bed toward the doorway. It hurt to breathe. I held on to my side and braced myself trying not to put any more pressure on my ribs. Once I got to the doorway of the bedroom, I managed to get to my feet and into the hallway, and I literally slid down the stairs into the living room. With only the outside street light filtering into the downstairs, I stumbled into the kitchen and reached for the phone on the wall.

I held on to my side as I slid down the wall to sit on the floor. I did not know who I was going to call. If I called the police, Jeff would be put in jail, and our kids would be embarrassed and hurt. Maybe I'll call the domestic violence hotline. That's right, I'll call the hotline, I thought. I turned on the light, fumbled around, and found the White Pages on the bottom shelf in the butler's pantry. The number was on the first page, and I dialed it. I cut off the light and resumed my position on the floor in total darkness. The woman on the line asked if I was in danger. I said no. I explained that my husband had hit me and that I thought that I had hurt him. I told her that I didn't want to call the police. She recommended that I go to a hospital emergency room. I declined and said that I would call my own doctor. She urged me to call my doctor right away. I agreed and hung up. I called my doctor's office and left a message with the answering service. Within minutes, my doctor called me back and told me to go to the emergency room. Again, I declined but said that it wasn't that bad and that I would go the next morning.

She told me that it was a crime for my husband to hit me and that I needed to report the incident, go on record, and get protection. She wanted to see me at her office on Monday. I told her that I would come to her office but that right then I was tired and just needed to lie down.

I slept on the couch that night and awoke early the next morning to take Christine to work. Then I went to the hospital emergency care center.

The waiting room was empty, and I was glad that no one could hear me explain to the intake clerk why I was there. She showed no visible reaction to my story but recommended I go to the Women's Shelter near the County Courthouse after the examination. I promised that I would go. The X-ray results showed cracked ribs and internal bleeding. I was directed to stay in bed and wear a body brace. I didn't go to church with the family the next day. I stayed in bed and watched infomercials. It was the first time in a long time that I skipped going to church.

A few days later, I went to see my doctor, who encouraged me to file a petition for a protection from abuse. I told her that Jeff was fine now and that he had apologized. He had assured me that it wouldn't happen again and that if it did, I could go ahead and file the petition. She said that wasn't good enough, because, the next time, he could kill me. Maybe, just maybe, she was right.

Jeff's forearm swelled up considerably during the next few days, and he complained that it stayed sore and was constantly throbbing. I recommended that he go and get it checked out. He did that and came home with his forearm in a cast. It was broken. He took his injury in stride as though it were a sports injury. Without words, we knew it was his punishment for hitting me. He promised that he would keep his commitment to Christ, me, and the family, and that he would not go out drinking.

To be on the safe side, I went to the Women's Shelter that week. The staff explained how to file a petition for a protection from abuse order and suggested that I get counseling. I said okay but didn't seek counseling because I didn't think we needed it. I was confident that Jeff would get his act together once I threatened to file for the protection order. I was sure of it.

Over the next few weeks, I had trouble sleeping and was in constant pain. The rib brace was uncomfortable, and it was painful to take deep breaths. Every morning, I felt a new pain in a different region of my torso and couldn't understand how I could hurt in an area that Jeff hadn't punched. I called my doctor who explained that because of the internal injuries I sustained, each day blood would travel to a different area around my ribs and torso causing discomfort. Eventually, the pain subsided, and I was able to get out of bed without bracing myself.

I started having nightmares. In one dream, demons were trying to kill me at work with a time bomb set for 9:30 a.m. The three demons kept checking the timer on my desk to see if the bomb was still set to go off. Three times they checked, and on the third attempt an angel picked me up out of my seat and carried me up towards the ceiling into another part of the building, and I was saved.

In another dream, Jeff was chasing me and wanting to kill me. I was in a continuous loop of running, crying, and screaming over and over. The dream would not end. I would wake up screaming and covered in sweat.

***

Our marriage was in deep trouble. Even though the warning signs were obvious, I refused to take them seriously. I believed that our marital difficulties were just a temporary setback for us and that we would overcome them. We were prospering financially, the kids were healthy, and we both enjoyed our work. We enjoyed the small luxuries that came along with our successful careers. We continued in our daily tasks of family life, and Jeff continued to preach. A lot of his messages to the congregation were about overcoming life's obstacles and obtaining financial success. I listened to him preach and offered positive feedback whenever he asked me how he had done.

For most of the year, we wore the masks of denial and shame. I say "we" because I felt partly responsible for the charade. I kept Jeff's struggles a secret, not wanting to disclose the truth of what I thought was a drinking problem or the truth of the anguish I felt inside. The masks we wore fit us well.

We attended the annual Valentine's Day dinner event sponsored by area churches and looked like the ideal couple.

When friends asked about his broken arm, he jokingly said that he hurt it playing around with me.

When our son graduated from Army boot camp, we drove down to South Carolina to attend the ceremonies. It was a pleasant trip with no drama.

We attended my 20th high school reunion. It was a grand affair. Jeff was asked to give the invocation and prayer of thanksgiving for the meal. I was filled with haughty pride at having a tall, handsome, and successful husband. I remembered being teased as a teenager and used this event to prove to my former classmates that I wasn't so homely after all and that I was pretty enough to catch such a good-looking man as Jeff. Yes! We did look good!

However, the trip to Orlando for our 20th wedding anniversary was quite different. The masks came off. Jeff did not come home the night before the trip but called me at seven o'clock in the morning to let me know that he'd meet me at the airport. He told me to pack certain items for him. I asked a neighbor to take me to the airport with our bags, and I was quite annoyed the entire flight. Jeff appeared relaxed and in a good mood. I didn't want to create any tension by badgering him about where he had been the night before. He knew I was upset, and he tried to be pleasant.

Once we arrived in Florida, Jeff started drinking. I had planned a tight schedule of activities that included a helicopter sightseeing tour, a mystery theatre dinner show, and a visit to Pleasure Island. I had made preparations for a fun trip, and I was going to make sure that nothing would spoil it, not even my own nagging sense of dread.

When we arrived at Pleasure Island, I made a mental note that the jazz club was close to the main entrance. Jeff liked jazz, and I hoped that he would want to sit there for a while and enjoy some music. When I reminded him later that night where the jazz club was, he accused me of being there before with another man. He demanded to know who I had been there with, and in his rage, left me at the club. He had the keys to the rental car. I was stranded. I sat alone at a table in the back of the club and watched as couples came in and out, holding hands, hugging, kissing, smiling, and whispering in each others' ears. I envied those couples.

I sat there for almost two hours until it dawned on me that I could take a taxi back to the hotel. As I pulled myself together to leave, Jeff appeared at the doorway. He was drunk. I could barely stand the smell but was grateful that he came back for me. He didn't say a word as he tried to find the car in the massive parking lot. I watched as he staggered between the rows of cars, and I hesitated to point out where the car was for fear of another unwarranted accusation. He insisted on driving, and I let him.

Over the next six weeks, Jeff stayed out all night three times. When he returned home, he would sulk and be depressed for a day or two and then bounce back to his vibrant self. He'd pick up where he left off, and life would go back to normal for us. On one occasion, I called Bishop Jones and complained that Jeff hadn't come home the previous night. The Bishop told me that he would approach Jeff and that I should not do anything at that point. I trusted Bishop Jones and obeyed his instruction. I believed the Bishop had our best interests at heart, and pretty soon, Jeff seemed like he was back on track.

At Christmas, Jeff bought the kids what they wanted and treated me to several gifts. I wondered if the gifts were peace offerings for his poor behavior throughout the year. I accepted the gifts anyway. A few days later, he disappeared again, and this time, his son wanted some answers. I told my son that I suspected his father might be using drugs, but I wasn't sure. I also told Jeff, Jr., that Bishop Jones was trying to help us.

On New Year's Day, Jeff disappeared again and didn't return until the next morning, just in time to take our son back to his military base in Fort Eustis, Virginia. Jeff and I took turns driving down, and I did not bring up his absence while our son and two of his fellow Army friends were in the van. However, I drove all the way home without stopping, and during the five hour stretch, I told Jeff just how disgusted I was with him and that I wanted answers. He was silent most of the time. The only consolation he could give me was to promise that he would do better and to ask me to just be patient with him.

***

Reflection:

The pressures of being a pastor's wife and having to keep secrets took their toll on me. At a meeting for ministers' wives, we were told to be our husbands' cheerleaders and his number one fans. I never forgot that advice and tried my best to be supportive of Jeff. During the times of conflict and struggle between us, I always thought in the back of my mind that "this, too, shall pass." Whenever he was depressed about something that was going on with the church ministry or its members, I tried to encourage him and offer words of assurance that everything would be all right. I really had his best interests at heart and wanted to get back to the good times we had shared together in the past. But by the end of 1995, the struggles lingered on, and I was tired of being a pastor's wife. My desire to serve in that role had died.

7
One Boulder at a Time

"And Jesus said unto them, Because of your unbelief: for verily I say unto you, If ye have faith as a grain of mustard seed, ye shall say unto this mountain, Remove hence to yonder place; and it shall remove; and nothing shall be impossible unto you." – Matthew 17:20

"You may have to fight a battle more than once to win it." – Margaret Thatcher

A few days into January 1996, a major snow storm hit and shut down most of the Northeast. Schools, businesses, and government agencies were closed. It was one of the biggest snow storms ever. We were also hit by a severe inner storm that nearly shut our family down.

Jeff confessed to me that he'd been using crack cocaine for the past year and he wanted to get tested. He asked for my help. My mind flashed back to our Florida trip and the night he left me at the jazz club. When we had gotten back to the hotel, he wanted to have sex. I didn't want to, but I gave in. It was just after one of his disappearing acts, and I felt uneasy about sleeping with him because I didn't know where he had been or if he had been sleeping with someone else. I didn't want to start a fight or possibly get beat up while we were on vacation, so I acquiesced.

I was stunned by his admission. I felt empathy for him and told him that I would help. I immediately went into rescue mode and outlined a plan of action. First, he would have to get tested for sexually transmitted diseases and HIV/AIDS. Second, he would have to talk to Bishop Jones, Al Motley, and anyone else he respected who had a direct pipeline with the Lord. He must have someone in his life who would pray for him and with him, someone who would hold him accountable for his actions.

I remembered the radio talk shows about marriage and families in crisis that I used to listen to on my commute to and from work. I remembered the self-help books I had read by prominent Christian and non-Christian leaders about marriage and relationships. One of the key steps to change is to first admit that you have a problem. I believed Jeff had realized that he had a problem and was now willing to address it. We knelt by the bed and prayed for a long while. Afterwards, I looked up phone numbers for public health clinics and Christian rehab centers. Many businesses were closed, so I waited a day or two to schedule appointments. Jeff was satisfied that I agreed to help him and was willing to do whatever needed to be done.

A week later, I was in criminal court filing for a protection from abuse order. We had agreed months ago that if ever I felt threatened by him I would file for the protection order, and I reminded him that I needed it in order to feel safe. I was relieved when Jeff found out that his test results were negative. So there was no threat to my health and safety on that end, but I still needed some form of protection if things got out of control. Jeff was served the papers while I was at work one day, and he immediately left the house. He came back the following day in a good mood and acted as though nothing had happened. It was as though he had come back from the dead. He burst into the house and was excited about some new "venture." He insisted that I transfer $1,000 into his account. I didn't know why, but I was accustomed to Jeff's cooking up some new business idea or project that required an outlay of money in order to get started.

In years past, Jeff had gotten involved with Amway, pyramid schemes, bulk food distribution, and other self-directed enterprises. Some were successful for a while, and others failed almost immediately, but at least he pursued whatever endeavor sparked his interest. I wasn't going to throw a wrench into his "big surprise" for the family. As long as he was working, bringing in money, and paying our bills, I wouldn't protest or make any waves. When he worked, he worked hard and pushed himself. I did not want to discourage him while he was so upbeat and determined to fight this problem. I just wanted peace in my home. So, I didn't argue and transferred the money into his account.

Jeff had just signed a contract for a new house. He told me that he wanted a fresh start, and that's why he needed the money. He had been working extra hard to prove to me that he would not succumb to drug addiction and that with God's help he had the power to change. He convinced me that I would love the house and that it was what we needed to revitalize and restore our family. When he took me to see the model home I was in awe as we walked through the huge structure. All I could think about was how I was going to clean all of it. He promised me that the move would be good for us. I was annoyed that he made the decision without my input and wondered why he made such an important and costly commitment like new home construction. He found a buyer for our current home, and the wheels were in motion. Jeff had always had big dreams, and I was along for the ride.

***

I was suspicious about Jeff's newfound enthusiasm and was afraid that it would not last. I called the employee assistance program counselor from work, got a referral for a family lawyer, and made an appointment. The lawyer explained state laws regarding separation, custody, and divorce. I told him about the problems we were having, and he recommended that we get marriage counseling and individual counseling for his drug and alcohol abuse issues and possibly anger management. I was willing to do whatever I needed to do in order to save the marriage. I told him that we were in the process of building a new home and that another payment was coming up within a few days. I was afraid that, if our marital problems persisted, we would lose our earnest money. He recommended that I put those things on hold for the time being. I was afraid to put a hold on everything and did not take his advice. We put down the next deposit. A few days later and unbeknownst to Jeff, I called the real estate broker to inquire about possibly canceling our offer to purchase and was told that it was too late to withdraw.

The protection from abuse order came through, and it was granted for one year. The protection from abuse order or restraining order allows police to arrest the abusive partner only if a violation is reported. I had one year to see if things would get better. My stomach was in knots, and the nightmares started up again. I told Jeff that I was afraid to go any further with the house purchase unless he was willing to go to marriage counseling. Jeff agreed to see Bishop Jones. Our first session was a disaster. For every accusation I made, he counteracted with an explanation. He deliberately sabotaged the meeting by trying to prove that my issues were baseless. He claimed that we could handle our own issues and that it was our business and no one else's. Bishop Jones recommended that we meet again.

I continued my search for a qualified Christian therapist and a spiritual treatment center for his alcohol abuse. I went to bookstores and pored over the self-help section for books about marriage. I remembered that all sin first comes to us through the mind, so I purchased the book, *Battlefield of the Mind*, by Joyce Meyer. This was one of many books that started me on the road to recovery.

By March, the foundation of the house had been poured and construction was well underway. Jeff's enthusiasm was contagious. We were approved for a mortgage, and we picked out paint colors, patterns, carpet, and fixtures. The thought of starting over was intoxicating.

Even though excitement was brewing all around us, I still had a sense of dread about the whole thing. I felt like I was on the edge of a tall building inching my way along and hoping that the next stiff wind wouldn't sweep me over the edge and send me falling fifty stories to a bloody death. I wondered if God's grace would get me through this time. I questioned whether or not God was really working on my behalf behind the scenes. I asked myself why God would bring me this far along in the marriage to have it all crumble in my hands on the eve of a possible breakthrough. I told myself to hold on just a little longer to see what the end would be.

Jeff was upbeat and active again at church. We regularly attended Bible study meetings and worship services. Set Free Christian Fellowship had pretty much disintegrated when some transplanted members who did not like Jeff's authoritative style planted seeds of discourse among the other members. Jeff became discouraged and recommended to the faithful few members to attend another church in the neighborhood. Jeff decided to close the doors of the church he founded and discontinued services.

Jeff and I continued to have counseling sessions with the Bishop. The Bishop instructed me not to discuss our marital problems with anyone at the church. He explained that he didn't want the congregation to know that we were having problems. And he specifically told me not to discuss anything with his wife. I wondered who would be my spiritual support. Who would pray for me? Who would cry with me? Who would understand? Who would listen to my tales of woe? I felt abandoned again just as I did when my father left my apartment without waiting for me to open the door. I had to get help for myself on my own.

I began individual counseling sessions through my job's employee assistance program and met with a woman therapist during my lunch hour. On our first meeting, I filled out a questionnaire about why I was there, and we chatted briefly. During the second visit, the counselor suggested that I continue to maintain control of large amounts of the money and make joint decisions that affect the entire family. She told me that I should concentrate on what's best for the future of the family and for my own health and well being, including protection from diseases. She explained that I should affirm positive behavior with Jeff.

By the third session, I had decided to change therapists. I felt that she didn't possess the same sense of urgency and intensity that I had. She gave me good advice, but it was soft and idealistic. I needed a counselor who would give me specific directions on what to do in a crisis. I needed a step-by-step action plan and searched for another counselor who knew how to deal with his violent and destructive behaviors. I did not want a counselor who only focused on ideas. I wanted hard and tangible tools that would force a change.

I decided that it might be wise to legally separate and called the legal services hotline number for information regarding the state's law on legal separation. And that time, I listened intently. I gave Jeff an ultimatum and told him that he'd better change or else I would leave.

I told my mom about his drinking, his threats, and the fights, and she called me weak. She told me that I had always been docile and timid. I told her that Jeff asked me to give him $1,900. I gave him the money just to avoid a fight and to get him out of the house. After he left, I felt relieved and very, very tired. That incident only proved her point. However, I was determined to prove to my mother that I wasn't as mild-mannered and meek as she thought. I wanted to stand up for myself and prove to my mother that I was indeed a strong, black woman just like her.

I dreamt that night that the Lord told me to leave Jeff. The next morning, I filed a police report and spoke with the assistant district attorney about the threats and the extortion for money. I later called my doctor because I had unexplained stomach pain. When I told her about what had been going on at home, she recommended that I get psychiatric help. I was insulted and did not do as she suggested. I'm not the crazy one, I thought. Jeff is the crazy one.

Jeff had been gone for about three days, and our daughter Christine and her boyfriend went looking for him. I had checked our banking transactions record and located the part of town where the most frequent and last ATM bank transactions took place. Christine found our van parked on a residential street and decided to wait nearby to see if her father would come out of any of the homes on the street.

Their detective work paid off. After a few hours, Christine was devastated when she saw her father come out of a house in the wee hours of the morning. Her boyfriend went into the house and discovered that it was a crack house. I was not surprised when Christine told me the story. I was only saddened that she had to find out that her father was using drugs. I told her to come home and leave him alone and that there was nothing she could do. When Jeff finally returned home after being gone for a week, I called a family meeting.

During the meeting, Jeff was contrite and said that he intended to get help for his problem. He agreed to be accountable to someone other than me about his drug use. It was not the best resolution, but I was temporarily satisfied since it involved accountability to someone else. I felt a sense of hope and relief in sharing the responsibility of being my brother's keeper. I believed that the church hierarchy should bear some of the burden in ensuring that its members and leaders honor a code of ethics. The pastors, bishops, and other honchos should be responsible for the conduct of the laity. If one church member suffers, so does the rest of the church.

And if Jeff had a problem then we should all help him with it. The Bible says in Galatians 6:1-2, "Brethren, if a man be overtaken in a fault, ye which are spiritual, restore such an one in the spirit of meekness; considering thyself, lest thou also be tempted. Bear ye one another's burdens, and so fulfil the law of Christ."

I encouraged Jeff to call his Christian male friends. I wanted him to talk to someone who would understand and empathize with him and not judge him. I had hoped that they would cover the multitude of sins plaguing him. The Bible says in 1 Peter 4:8, "And above all things have fervent charity among yourselves: for charity shall cover the multitude of sins." Our family was hurting, and I believed Jeff was sincere about getting the help he needed. But, as long as I was told to keep silent, I couldn't do much except pray for him. Jeff didn't want anyone to know about his personal problems, and my hands were tied. I had been forbidden to talk about it with anyone. I told Jeff that I loved him and that I was sorry that there was no one he trusted. Only one or two of his friends responded to the call. It seemed as though he was being shunned. I was very hurt and could not understand why his so-called friends would not reach out to him and help. I could see the pain in Jeff's face. I could feel his broken heart. I cried for my husband because I sensed his isolation.

I had another dream and the Lord told me again to leave. There had been no progress. I asked the Lord, "When?" I did not hear an answer about when I should make my move. I needed more information. I thought, "How could I leave Jeff to fight his battle alone? How could I desert him when he needed my help?" I started feeling anxious and wondered if staying would put my life in danger if he were overcome with rage while under the influence of drugs and alcohol. I asked God again, "When, Lord, should I leave?" God was silent. So, I waited and didn't move.

In the next few months, I called a lawyer and asked questions to help me determine what was at stake. I started attending ALANON meetings and began individual counseling sessions with a new therapist.

On June 1, 1996, Jeff and I argued, and he started breaking things in our bedroom. I did not realize that my nephew Eric heard the argument and was on the phone crying to his mother, my youngest sister. On the other end of the line, LaShawn heard the commotion and called the police. A short while later, someone banged on the front door. Jeff went downstairs to find two police officers at the door who said that they were responding to a call. One officer stayed downstairs and questioned Jeff. The other officer came upstairs into our bedroom and started questioning me. He saw the disarray in the room, the broken items, and asked me what happened. I confirmed that Jeff had made the mess and that I had a protection from abuse order on record. The officers arrested him on the spot. I supposed that, since children were in the house and that I had an existing protection from abuse order, they had no choice but to arrest Jeff. I never went downstairs. I didn't have the heart to look at my husband being taken away in handcuffs like some kind of criminal. But in the eyes of the law, he was a criminal.

I had hoped that this incident might wake him up and make him realize that our situation was serious and that everything was at stake.

He was in jail for a few days, and when he got home he was very remorseful and apologetic. He told me that he was so angry with me that he crushed his wedding band but later thought better of it, and he promised to have it restored. I told him that I thought it would be best if we separated for a while. I was sick of his promises and wanted to be left alone to think about what I needed to do next. We would need to move into the new house soon, and I was really conflicted about it all.

Jeff packed a few things and went to stay with a relative for a short while.

While Jeff was gone Eric started acting out, and I could not control him. His anger and defiance left me with little recourse. I had to send him to live with his father. Eric had been with us for a little over a year, and I thought he was making good progress. I suspect that my conflict with Jeff made matters worse for my nephew, and I felt very sorry that I was a poor example. I had let him down.

***

My new counselor, Larry, offered sound advice and recommended that I participate in group therapy sessions with other abuse victims. He also recommended that I read the book *Men are from Mars and Women are from Venus* to help me understand the differences in the way men and women think. Larry suggested that I start a journal and that I do things to help alleviate stress, like listening to music and visualizing being in a serene place. He encouraged me to continue making joint decisions with Jeff, who had lately been extremely calm, and for me to think about what's making him so calm.

I believed Jeff finally took me seriously about leaving him, and he didn't want to rock the boat when he was so close to having his dream come true. He wanted desperately to move into that house. I wanted my husband to see his dream fulfilled and not be considered a loser. His success was my success. In spite of everything we had gone through, I really loved Jeff and wanted nothing but the best for him and the best for us. But I needed to learn how to take care of myself, and that was why I was in therapy.

***

Reflection:
> *As recorded in my diary:*
> *On April 4, 1996, I prayed this prayer to the Lord –*

"*Dear Jesus,*

I am not happy with the way I respond to Jeff's using drugs. Because I get so volatile, he says Christianity hasn't changed me. I'm too emotional. When I'm angry I...

raise my voice, yell, cry, become argumentative, I resist his sexual advances, and don't want to have sex with him and I either "fight" him and get hurt or I'll roll over and submit and hate him for forcing me.

"Lord, help me. How am I to respond to him? If I go quietly, will he abuse me or if I yell will he leave me. What can I do to end all of this madness? I need help. Love,

Lynn

Lord – come quickly or take me home."

8
Moving In

"God does not offer us a way out of the testings of life. He offers us a way through, and that makes all the difference."
– W. T. Purkiser

It was moving day, and things were bustling. Jeff had coordinated everything from getting our family and friends to help, to ensuring that the closing sale transaction of our old house went smoothly. The closing on the new house hit a snag when Jeff discovered some undisclosed fees listed on the HUD-1 form and insisted that the charges be removed by the mortgage broker. Jeff's calm composure and firm resolve reminded me of why I admired and loved him so much. He refused to be manipulated by people and had a strong business savvy that was rare in most people. He was always one step ahead, and I felt confident that he'd handle any underhanded dealings made by bankers, lawyers, and dishonest businessmen. After the broker arranged to have the fees removed, we were back on track and on our way to move in.

By late evening, we were in our new home and were thoroughly exhausted. It was exhilarating, and we rejoiced in finally making a dream come true. It was wonderful seeing Jeff so excited about picking out new furniture and window treatments. He was involved in every aspect of the house, and I was just as happy watching him. I believed that with this change Jeff would be renewed and energized enough to crawl out of the slump that had propelled him to use drugs, and I prayed that he would continue and strengthen his walk with the Lord.

Our sprawling 4,000 square foot home had four bedrooms, a three-car garage, and a back patio and deck overlooking a quarter of an acre of lush green grass. Jeff had an office, and I had my own vanity and sitting area in our massive master bedroom. The kitchen and family room offered an exquisite view of the backyard, and the planted bushes and shrubs around the front and sides of the house enhanced its elegance. The cathedral and vaulted ceilings allowed an enormous amount of light into the house, and I simply loved all the open space. Our investment to upgrade to cherry wood kitchen cabinets and a partial brick front increased the value of the home immediately, and I was pleased that Jeff had the foresight to add those options. Jeff brought a riding lawn mower and mulch and turned out to be a pretty good gardener. I was proud of him and was thrilled that he was happy.

In the next several days, the welcoming committee came by with a basket of goodies, and we got a chance to meet some of our neighbors. We visited a few neighborhood churches, but none appealed to Jeff. He occasionally drove all the way to Philadelphia to attend church services. I preferred to stay local, but I deferred to him on that issue. Wherever he wanted to go to church was fine with me just as long as he went.

At the end of July on a hot Sunday afternoon, Jeff went for a drive and didn't return home until the next evening. I had missed work that day because I didn't have a babysitter. After that incident, I made quick friends with my next door neighbor who agreed to watch Michelle if ever I got into a pinch. She was a stay-at-home mom pregnant with her second child. I was grateful that she was glad to help.

I became increasingly aware that Jeff was slipping back into the abyss of depression, and I started writing more in my journal. Some of my writings were frantic and urgent, and some were clear and concise. I'll share a couple of those entries here.

August 8, 1996 – Entry

"It's near that time of year. When ever August 10th or so comes around Jeff goes into a blitz. I'm trying hard not to concern myself with him or be obsessed with what he does. I want to leave – to escape his tyranny, his selfishness, but I'm afraid to leave his love. Lord, God, please open my eyes. Help me see "enough" to leave." He went through a blitz on August 12.

Over the years, I could predict erratic behavior that seemed to occur almost every year in the month of August. That's why I mentioned the annual "blitz." It usually manifested itself by an unexplained absence and irrational or violent behavior, and it usually occurred sometime in early August. Sometimes the blitz skipped a year or two. I believed that something traumatic happened in Jeff's childhood during August but was never able to confirm my hypothesis.

August 28, 1996 – Entry

I need to reassess this situation. I need to list the pros and the cons of staying in the marriage. My heart says stay, but my head says leave. Michelle needs her dad, and he needs her. If I stay, the chances for Jeff's complete recovery from crack cocaine are slim. If I leave they might increase or he might hit rock bottom. As long as I'm around he'll depend on me. If I leave, he'll have to depend on God or fall. I'm afraid to leave. I'm afraid to be alone. But when I'm angry at the results of his behavior I become vigilant, strong, almost crazy and determined to leave. But then the dust settles. And I'm back in the same boat, on the

> *same merry go round. STOP. I want – no – I need to get off.*

And, then there were moments of absolute clarity.

August 29, 1996 – Entry

Lord, help me know and do what I must do according to your Word.

We continued our ruse, and Jeff and I entertained family and friends in our new home like any normal suburban couple. We would ride our bikes around the development, go hiking in the park down the road, and visit with our neighbors. We'd mow the lawn, tend to our flowers, and play catch with our daughter out back. I wore the mask of complacency and endured maintaining the charade of a happy and prosperous marriage.

However, Jeff and I were both snapped to reality when one of our neighbors committed suicide. The husband had been laid off from work and was depressed. His wife worked to make ends meet, and we could sense the tension between the couple. One night while his wife and two young children were asleep, he went into the garage, got into the car, started the engine and died from its emissions. The next morning, the entire community was shocked to hear the tragedy of such a beautiful couple. However, Jeff and I realized that that couple could easily have been us.

***

My grandmother died on November 5, 1996, and my mother asked me to help her with funeral arrangements. I took off from work that Thursday and went to Philadelphia. I returned home late that evening and was giving Michelle a bath when I asked her how her day was. She recounted the events of the day, which included riding in the truck with her daddy and some lady to get bar juice. Bar juice? Lady? I thought what in the world is bar juice and who in the world was this lady? I started to fume. After putting Michelle to bed, I confronted Jeff. He told me that he just gave some woman a ride and that he went to the liquor store. I started yelling at him. He told me to lower my voice or else he might do something that we'd both regret. Then he left. I got scared. I was afraid he'd actually come back high and do something harmful to me. I couldn't take that risk. I packed a few things to last a couple of days, woke up my little girl, and headed for Philadelphia.

I drove over 35 miles on sheer adrenaline, and it must have been just after midnight when I pulled into the Fairfield Inn parking lot near the Philadelphia airport. I didn't have a plan and didn't know where to turn. My embarrassment about my predicament kept me sitting in my car for a few moments while I thought of a gut-wrenching story to tell the clerk at the check-in counter of the Inn. A young woman who was checking in at the same time heard me say that the nightly rate was a little more than what I was willing to pay. I leaned in to speak softly to the clerk without being overheard and tried to negotiate a cheaper rate. I told her I was running away from a dangerous situation and was looking for a place just for the night. The hotel clerk apologized and said she couldn't accommodate us at a cheaper rate and told me to try Motel 6 next door. I got back into my car and sat for a moment trying to decide if I should go back home or go to the establishment next door. The tears began to well in my eyes. I wiped them quickly before my child could see my reflection in the rear view mirror.

Then the young woman I had seen inside the lobby walked out and appeared to be looking for someone. She saw me sitting in the car and came over to us. She could see that the back seat of my car was packed with a six-year-old, some clothes, a pillow, and a blanket. I rolled down the window. She said she had overheard my conversation and offered that we stay in the room with her for the night. I thanked her for her generosity and told her that I would get a room at Motel 6. She persisted and asked if I was sure and if I would be safe. Again, I told her how much I appreciated her kindness and told her that I was sure we would be okay and that tomorrow I would sort things out. I never forgot the extraordinary courage of this young woman who approached us and offered to help. I wish I had known more people like her.

I got a room that night at Motel 6 and ended up staying there for three days. Christine and Jeff, Jr. came to stay with us for a couple of those days. It was on our wedding anniversary that I was convinced that I should leave their father once and for all and went window shopping for apartments. Jeff had been pleading with me to come back home and made more promises. Michelle had already missed a day away from school, and I needed to get back to work, so I went back home just in time to attend Grandma's funeral.

My commute to work included an hour's drive each way, and I didn't like leaving and arriving home in the dark every day. It was depressing. Jeff took care of Michelle and made sure she had breakfast and got on the school bus every morning. He was there every day when she got off the school bus and cooked dinner for us every night. I'd arrive home exhausted only to do the same thing again the next day. But I enjoyed our new home and relished the weekends in all their tranquility. It was those quiet moments that caused me to reflect on how good God had been to me and my family over all those years. I believed that if I just held on a little longer He would give me what I always wanted -- a faithful husband who loved God with all his heart, mind, body, and soul, one who loved and cherished his wife. Did I ask for something too hard for God?

Jeff went out one night during the week and didn't get home until the next morning, which made me late for work. And on another morning, he didn't show up at all, and I had to call in sick. When I did get back to work, my boss, Chuck Ruoff, told me that I needed to get myself together. He said that my performance was slipping and that I needed to cancel all volunteer projects and focus on improving on the basic functions of my position. He told me that I needed to make some decisions about my home life and that too many times I was emotionally up and down because of Jeff. I hadn't realized that my home life was interfering with work and causing mood swings. I didn't want to believe his observation, and I thought I was doing quite well compared to what I was going through at home. I promised Chuck that I would do better. I confided in him that Jeff and I were having problems, and he told me that I needed to make some changes because it was interfering with my job.

One night shortly after Thanksgiving, I decided to ask Jeff where he had been and what he had been doing on those nights when he disappeared. He would come home smelling like dirt and perspiration and looking like some street bum. The smell reminded me of what I was trying to get away from -- the ghetto. I wanted to get away from the filthy streets, the squalor of poverty, the empty beer and liquor bottles, and discarded cigarette butts. I did not want to see the crack heads, the prostitutes, and drunks on every other corner. And he smelled just like all those things, and I despised him for going back to that environment. The stench made my stomach turn. I thought he wanted to do better than that. He had always told me that he did not want to be a part of that lifestyle, yet he was being drawn back to that very thing.

Jeff wasn't in the mood for discussions or for my nagging. He wanted to have sex. I resisted him and told him that I was still very angry about him not coming home that day so I could go to work. I told him that he needed to do better. He told me that he didn't want to hear my complaints and reminded me that I should be glad that he married me. He told me that he was the best thing that ever happened to me and that it was because of him that we were in that house. He reminded me of all the wise business decisions he had made in order for us to live as comfortably as we were living. He reminded me that I was always the one who tried to stifle his dreams. Like the time I questioned why he gave all of our wedding gift money to the visiting Pentecostal preacher who held revival services at my Uncle's church. And the time I cautioned him about buying a used Oldsmobile Toronado and how high the monthly payments would be or for taking out the various loans so he could start his business or other enterprises. He told me how I was always the one who tried to hold him back whenever he wanted to do something big, extravagant, or expensive that posed a financial risk to us. He told me that I was the one who stopped him from becoming rich. He claimed that it took money to make more money.

Surely, Jeff knew exactly what buttons to push to make me feel belittled and insignificant. He knew I would cringe under the weight of his accusations and second guess myself. Was it true that I ought to be glad that he married me? Maybe he was right. "NO!" He was not right. God had forgiven me for my sins. I could not allow Jeff to ridicule me or put me down.

Suddenly, I didn't want Jeff anywhere near me. By that time, he was in my face taunting me. I pushed him away from me and jumped out of bed. He rushed ahead of me and ran for the bedroom door, locked it, and grabbed me by both arms forcing me into my closet and onto the floor. I started struggling with him, and I could feel his body tense. At some point, he hit me, and since I didn't want to get hit again, I gave in. I knew that the only way to get back at him was to not show any pleasure at his touch and to just lay there as he forced himself on me. I knew what buttons to push, too.

And, as I laid there pinned under him, I showed no reaction except for the tear drops that rolled from each eye into my ears. He held me down and raped me. I wouldn't scream. It was my own fault for not leaving him years ago. I kept turning my head from side to side trying to avoid coming into contact with any part of his face as he tried to kiss me. The back of my neck started to itch and burn from the constant friction against the carpet fibers. I could feel my head start to sweat and my hair begin to contract at the first sign of moisture. My forehead stung as the salty beads of perspiration from his face dripped on me and rolled into my ears. I hated him for forcing me. I just hated him. After he was done, he got up and walked out of the closet, closed the door, and barricaded me inside.

I wiped myself dry with my underwear and tried not to make a sound. I felt really sorry for myself and lay there for a long time. I wondered how much longer I could stay in this beautiful house, as miserable as I was. This was not the way it was supposed to be. This house was supposed to make us happy. Why had I gone along with the whole idea? I have got to get out of here, I thought. And I should've left a long time ago. But it was much too late in the night to leave, and I was too tired to go anywhere. All I wanted to do was curl up in my bed and pull the covers over my head. I wanted to block out the entire world and disappear. But I couldn't. I had a child to take care of. I have to live at least for her sake. When he finally opened the door and released me, all I could do was crawl into bed and go to sleep.

The next morning, I sat on the edge of the bed not wanting to get up to face another day. I was so tired. I was tired of worrying about Jeff and what he was doing. I had done all I could do to be a good wife, and I was exhausted. I was a walking zombie just going through the motions. I would drive to work and not remember if I drove through a red light or not. I couldn't concentrate and wondered how I got through the work day and back home again. Day in and day out. I kept up the farce for as long as I could.

And one morning as I dreaded getting up, I realized that something had to change, and it was not going to be Jeff. I slid to my knees like a wet rag sliding off the edge of the sink onto the floor. I assumed the position, but the words wouldn't come out. How many times had I prayed for a miracle? How many times had I prayed for my family, friends, and other people through their hard times? But this time, I didn't know what to say. All I could muster were a few words. "Please God. Help me. Please God. Change me."

A week before Christmas I looked at a few more apartments and found a complex in a suburb outside of Chester, Pennsylvania, that was close to my job and only one block from an elementary school. The apartment manager was a very pleasant man who assured me that I would have no problem getting an apartment. He took my application and deposit and allowed me to pick the unit I wanted.

A couple of days later, the manager called me at work and told me that my application was approved and that I could move in whenever I was ready. I asked him to hold the unit since I wasn't ready to move in yet, and he agreed. I wanted to wait until after the Christmas holiday and also to give Jeff another chance to get his act together.

Preparations were being made, and my mother was coming to visit for Christmas. I had planned to celebrate in our brand new house and didn't want anything to go wrong. We bought a beautiful live tree, put up decorations, and wrapped presents. I was glad that my mother was able to see how much we had achieved in spite of our turbulent marriage. I wanted her to see that we could achieve anything when we worked together as a team. I was proud of myself, and I wanted her to be proud of me, too. I was sorry, though, that my father couldn't see his "slim goodie" achieve so much. "Slim goodie" was my dad's pet name for me. He and my mom had separated in 1982 because of his alcoholism, and he died from throat cancer in 1992.

I had set aside a few hundred dollars for the kids as Christmas gifts and placed the money in my Bible for safekeeping. It was early on Christmas Eve, and everything was just about ready. We needed a few things from the supermarket, so Jeff had to run out. It snowed that night, and by Christmas morning he still had not returned. I did not panic or worry and proceeded as though nothing was wrong. I cooked breakfast, and we opened presents. When I went to my Bible to get the money for Christine and Jeff, Jr., it was gone. I was so stunned I couldn't speak. I simply could not believe it. Not because Jeff took the money from me, but because he took it away from our children. And he took it on Christmas Day. How low could he get? How desperate was he to feed his drug habit that he would spoil one of the most reverent and most holy days of the year? What gall. What audacity.

Later that evening, he came home as if nothing had happened. He bustled about as though he had just gotten off work by shaking the snow off his clothes and taking his boots off in the garage for fear of tracking the dirty snow into the house. He apologized for missing all the festivities of the morning and for taking the money. He promised to replace it the next day. We all sat down to dinner together and not a word was said about his disappearance. I had been conditioned not to confront him for fear of starting a fight.

Two days later I went back to Rose Tree Apartments, put down a security deposit on the unit, and scheduled a move-in date for January 25. Now, I had to figure out when and how I was going to tell Jeff that I was moving out.

***

Reflection:

Learn all you can about the signs of drug use and addiction before it's too late.

9
Time to Move Out

"To every thing there is a season, and a time to every purpose under the heaven:" – Ecclesiastes 3:1

"When you know even for a moment that it's your time, then you can walk with the power of a thousand generations." – Bruce Cockburn

It was six days into the New Year of 1997. I had just returned home from work and opened up a can of my favorite soup -- New England clam chowder. As I poured the hot chowder into a bowl and began to sip slowly, I mulled over how I was going to tell Jeff about my decision. After a minute or two, I mustered up the courage and told him that I was leaving him and would be taking Michelle with me. He began storming around the house, pacing back and forth from room to room, yelling that I wasn't going to take Michelle anywhere and that no court in the world would allow me to do so. He came into the kitchen and leaned over the table screaming in my face and said that it would be my fault if the family broke up and that once I left it couldn't be fixed. He said that our children would suffer and be ruined.

I started feeling very nauseated. Maybe the soup was bad. I didn't remember if I checked the expiration date. I began to sweat, and my hands were cool and clammy. I had the urge to throw up and ran into the bathroom, bent over the toilet bowl, gagged, dry heaved, and eventually threw up the soup. I was afraid that maybe I was making a big mistake in breaking up the family. I almost started to believe him. But then the images of him choking me came to mind.

I could feel my heart rate increase and was afraid that at any moment Jeff might snap and lash out at me or, worse yet, hurt Michelle. The thought of dying at his hands gave me courage. I knew that there was no way I was going to let him kill me in my house and leave my young child without a mother. As I became aware of what I was feeling and thinking, I also realized that that was why I had to leave this man. I ran cold water over my hands and wiped my hot forehead with a cool cloth.

I needed to get this over with and, after regaining my composure, I went back into the kitchen. I was ready to challenge him and was prepared to do it. I had a place to go and I had a plan. I felt empowered and confident in myself. I wasn't going to be dominated by him anymore. I spoke deliberately and slowly so that he would not misunderstand me. I explained as calmly as I could without showing any fear or hesitation that it would be best for me to leave, because I was afraid of him. I told him that we needed some time apart so he could focus on his recovery from crack cocaine. He said that we could work it out at home without my having to leave. I knew he was trying to get me to stay, but I told him that he needed help and that I needed to take care of myself.

But then I did something stupid. I added a "release clause." I hadn't planned it, but I was prepared to do anything at that point to have him accept my proposal and let me leave without a fight. I told him that once I got settled we could consider counseling and reconciliation, but until then, I had to leave. He calmed down a little and left the house. I took a deep breath and poured out the rest of the soup. I didn't have an appetite anymore, and all of a sudden New England clam chowder wasn't my favorite soup.

***

As I gazed at the clothes in my walk-in closet, I thought about what I could live without. I asked myself what items were essential. The pretty party dresses and elegant gowns would stay behind. Those high-heeled dress shoes weren't needed anymore. I only needed to pack the basics. Work clothes, a few dresses for church, winter clothing, and outerwear. Thick bathrobe, socks, and bedroom slippers. Fleece pajamas, yes. Sexy lingerie, no. Never knew I had so much stuff. Never knew how much I could live without.

Next, I went to Michelle's room. I would take all of her clothes, only a few of her favorite books, videos, and toys, and especially her baby blankets. I would buy her new games and entertainment so she wouldn't be reminded of what was left behind. She would focus on the new presents. We were about to celebrate her birthday in a couple of days, and I wanted her to be happy in spite of our circumstances.

I would have to buy a bed, a dinette set, sheets, dishes, pots, and pans -- just the basic stuff. Jeff Jr., Christine, and Linton, Christine's boyfriend, would help me move. I had made sure that Jeff wouldn't be home when we left, and he wasn't.

The two-bedroom apartment was perfect for us. It had a kitchen, a living room, one and a half bathrooms, a dressing area with ample closet space, and even a storage area assigned to our unit on the lower level. The building had a laundry room, so I didn't have to leave the building to wash our clothes. I didn't have to go up several flights of stairs with groceries or packages, and the parking lot was close to the main entryway. I was pleased that it met our needs and felt that I had made a good choice. The rent was $730 a month, and it was only 12 minutes from my job in Newtown Square.

I spent a lot of energy focusing on Michelle. We had moved the day before her seventh birthday, and I wanted to pamper her. I felt compelled to make up for moving her away from her new home, school, and friends. We celebrated her birthday at

Discovery Zone, had a pizza party, and opened plenty of gifts. Christine, Jeff, Jr. and a couple of Michelle's friends spent the day with us. Her father did not attend. It wasn't the first birthday party he had missed.

Two days after moving in, I wasn't feeling well. I had stomach cramps, diarrhea, and foot pain and went to see my medical doctor. She determined that I had a stomach virus, an inflamed breast bone, and a case of anxiety. She took several blood tests, including tests for STDs and HIV/AIDS, and asked me to come back in a week for the results. She also scheduled me for a mammogram and an upper GI series, and referred me to an orthopedist for my foot pain.

That afternoon, I found that the women's safe house was located within walking distance of the County Courthouse. I also called the Coalition Against Domestic Violence to get information on what services they provided, asked how they could help me, and asked what other agencies could help. I wanted to know where all the important places were in my new neighborhood just in case I needed to get out in a hurry.

On my follow-up doctor's visit, she insisted that I take my situation seriously. Even though the HIV/AIDS test came back negative, she reiterated that my overall health and medical problems were directly attributed to what was happening with Jeff and that I must continue counseling sessions. She told me to stop playing games with him and that the protection order was for real. She insisted that I have no contact with him, sexual or otherwise. She told me that I needed to take control of my physical health and that medication would help me stay focused while dealing with the problem. She scared me.

***

Our daily routine was beginning to take shape. I enrolled Michelle in her new school and signed her up for the before- and after-school care program. In the mornings, I would drive through the complex onto a connecting street to Michelle's school and drop her off at the before-school program located in a building adjoining the school. After school, she would be picked up by the day care staff, and I'd pick her up after I got off from work. During day care, she would have snacks, do her homework, and play inside or outside in the playground. I was relieved and grateful that things seemed to fall in place for us. You would think that I would be ecstatic and happy, but on most days I felt out of sorts, empty, and lonely.

Jeff called me several times a day, at the apartment and at work. The conversations were always the same. He wanted to know when I was coming home. Day after day, week after week, he'd have the same defeated sound in his voice as though he had been crying because he lost a fight and had given up. I would be exhausted from talking with him and felt emotionally drained by the time I ended each call. As the despair dripped from his lips my heart ached to help alleviate his pain. I wanted to take away his sorrow and rescue him. But sometimes the phone calls were scary. He would become enraged and scream into the phone, slam the receiver, and call back, and apologize. He swung on a pendulum going from despair and melancholy to anger and rage, and he couldn't seem to stop the wild swinging. He was Dr. Jekyll and Mr. Hyde.

I tried to take my mind off my problems and concentrate on something else. I made concerted efforts to improve my performance on the job but continued to operate on autopilot. I would come home from work exhausted, prepare a simple dinner for Michelle, and go over her homework. She adjusted well and didn't need a lot of help with her assignments. Even though I didn't have much of an appetite, I made sure she ate. Afterwards, I'd have her take a bath, and then I would go to bed. I didn't have energy to do anything else. Sometimes I would sleep 12 hours straight and still wake up just as tired as I had been the evening before. It was during my lapses in parenting that Michelle learned how to be self-sufficient. At seven years of age, she learned how to prepare simple meals like sandwiches, hot and cold cereals, and instant hot chocolate. She developed a routine, appeared content with her surroundings, and didn't complain or whine about missing her dad.

Jeff would occasionally ask to see Michelle, and I was willing to allow the visit whenever it was convenient for us. I made every attempt to be polite and not engage in lengthy or stressful conversations, because I was afraid he would take it out on Michelle. I never heard about any agitated behavior he might have displayed around her. I gave him a mental check mark and gold star for wanting to shield our daughter from his tirades.

By March, I was having dual counseling sessions - one with a minister and one with a therapist. The minister gave me advice from a Biblical standpoint for my spiritual well-being, and the psychotherapist was delving into my psyche to give me advice for my emotional well-being. It was a difficult balance, but I needed to address all facets of who I was. I could follow one set of instructions completely and totally ignore the other, or I could blend both philosophies into one perfect instruction manual that would lead to complete and total healing for my mind, body, and soul. I didn't believe the answer was that simple or that there was only one method. The hardest thing of all would be to navigate these competing theories. Would I ignore the Biblical principles of loving thy neighbor, forgiving thy brother, and bearing the fruit of long suffering? Would I protect myself and take Jeff to court, press charges, and have him locked up? Would I forgive him and reconcile or would I divorce him right away and not give it a second thought? It was going to be hard to decide which was the perfect way. So for now, let the games begin.

Proverbs 11:14 says, "Where no counsel *is*, the people fall: but in the multitude of counselors *there is* safety."

For the sake of simplicity, I'm going to call the person who gave me spiritual advice "the pastor." And I'll call the psychotherapist "Larry" (who's also mentioned earlier in

Chapter 7). They are both men. I address one by title and the other by name, but that is what I'm comfortable with, so bear with me.

What the pastor said

Jeff was desperate and would do anything to get me back, and he even agreed to meet with the pastor. The pastor couldn't believe the problem was as serious as I had claimed, because Jeff was so charming and unassuming. He recommended that we begin a path of reconciliation and that we consider going out on dates. He pointed out Bible verses that reinforced how Jeff was to treat me and how I should respond as a wife. Colossians 3:19 says, "Husbands, love your wives, and be not bitter against them," and Ephesians 5:22 says, "Wives, submit yourselves unto your own husbands, as unto the Lord."

The pastor also instructed me to:
1. go out with Jeff on Friday or Saturday nights;
2. help Jeff with the bills when possible;
3. ask God to help me control my tongue and my emotions; and
4. consider going back to live with Jeff in June.

This is how I saw it.

Number 1: I believed that since I was still married to him I had an obligation to fulfill his sexual needs regardless of whether I wanted to or not. I was used to being obedient and submissive. Jeff probably thought that if he wined and dined me, brought me gifts, and pressed the right buttons, he might get some "action" which would undoubtedly relieve some of his pent-up sexual frustrations. Good for him, bad for me. I would be exposed to sexually transmitted diseases or be lulled into a false sense of security disguised as a honeymoon. My interpretation of the pastor's recommendation to go out on dates with Jeff was a legal "booty call" in disguise. Well, that's how I saw it. But maybe that was not Jeff's ultimate goal at all. What do you think?

Number 2: If Jeff spent most of his money on drugs and came up a little short on paying bills, then I'd be responsible to help bail him out. Good for Jeff, bad for me. I'd lose the ability to financially sustain myself, especially if he became bankrupt, and would then be compelled to go back to him because I couldn't afford to live on my own. Just what a man would want, right? To be able to spend his money as he pleased and to get additional monies from his estranged wife was to his advantage, not mine. That's how I saw it.

Number 3: While asking God to control my tongue and temper Jeff wouldn't have to be confronted with my discontent. Another big break for him. If I kept my big mouth shut and didn't complain then he'd get the false impression that I was happy and content. Now we wouldn't want to rock the boat now would we? I'm starting to feel a little witchy right about now.

Number 4: My going back to the house would be the final victory for Jeff and the pastor. Their goal would be achieved, and they could boast of their conquest of subduing the "little woman" and proclaim that all was well. Great for them, bad for me. I'd be back where I started. That's how I saw it.

It looked like Jeff was getting the better end of the deal, while I settled for the occasional dinner and a movie routine. Somehow that just didn't seem right. I wrestled with that approach and thought long and hard about it. However, I trusted that the pastor knew what he was talking about. So I considered it.

What Larry said

Larry was very clear in his recommendations to me; he asked us to follow the path of nonviolence and to:

1. convey clear messages about what was expected during the weekend visits and to be careful and safe;

2. still keep boundaries;
3. make sure that both of us decided on events with no misperceptions;
4. understand that I was taking a risk if things went bad; and
5. change the way I cared about Jeff and not to rescue him.

During one counseling session with both of us, Jeff became so angry that he literally jumped up out of his seat, yelled at me and Larry, and stormed out of the session. Larry became afraid for me, asked me if I would be okay, and asked if he should call the police. I told him that I was accustomed to Jeff's loud outbursts and threats, that I would be fine, and that he should not worry. That's when Larry realized how much help we needed. He pushed for non-violence and equality in our marriage counseling sessions and recommended that I become knowledgeable about what I was up against. He recommended that I read several books, including *Codependency No More* and *Feel the Fear and Do It Anyway*. I also did my own book research on marriage, divorce, and remarriage from a Christian perspective.

Larry reminded me that I should allow Jeff to have regular interaction with Michelle, that we not criticize each other, and that we listen to each other. I listened intently to what he had to say and wrote things down. He worked with me on setting goals for our sessions that included:

1. knowing how I contributed to the marriage problems;
2. learning how to keep boundaries and limits and not to react;
3. learning about myself and why I do the things that I do; and
4. continuing therapy.

I rationalized that I could follow both lines of therapy from the spiritual and psychological points of view. I was determined to help my husband break free from his drug addiction and to stop the violence so we could get back to the work of raising our family and being successful. I wanted everything to be right between us and was willing to do my part.

I decided to start the trial period of living in the house with Jeff on the weekends as the pastor suggested. Pretty soon we were talking about reconciliation and made important decisions together. One decision was for me to look for a job closer to our home in Delaware. Another was to see a bankruptcy attorney and file for Chapter 13. Jeff had been on a spending spree since I moved out and had wasted a lot of money on drugs. He said that he was determined to get back on track and play catch-up to pay the bills on time.

I continued to stay at my apartment during the week, and by the end of March, I was going back to Delaware on the weekends. We agreed to some overall guidelines about our relationship and visits with Michelle. The new books I was reading inspired me to continue on this course even though I was afraid and had codependent tendencies. I was encouraged to demand those things that were rightfully mine and to venture beyond my comfort zone in spite of my anxiety.

I decided to start using my newfound strength. One night, Jeff called me to tell me that he forgot to pay the IRS bill. I asked him if he expected me to pay it. He said that he just wanted to let me know. I was becoming upset because I knew he expected me to pay his bill, but he said he would handle it. I suggested he borrow the money from someone or find some other remedy to pay the bill and that I would not cough up any money to pay it. I was already making payments on the second mortgage, business loan, and car note, as well as rent, utilities, and day care expenses that totaled over two thousand dollars a month. Jeff was used to me coming to the rescue and handling things, but this time I held firm and stood my ground. I would not take on the responsibility of paying a tax debt that he clearly owed. I felt good about standing my ground. Reading those books helped a great deal.

I continued to attend church on most Sundays. It was very awkward, because I couldn't talk to anyone in the congregation about what was happening to me or my marriage. Whenever someone asked me about Jeff, I had to lie with a smile on my face and say that he was fine. Since Jeff was considered a part of the leadership at the church, the pastor insisted that our marital problems be kept private and only be discussed with him.

The pastor didn't even trust his wife to talk to me about the abuse I had suffered at Jeff's hands. This put me in a terrible predicament. As I raised my hands in worship and sang hymns along with the chorus, tears would fall. People probably thought I was truly holy and that the tears I shed were tears of joy. I was actually crying out to God to please send me someone I could pray with, someone who would love me and care about what I was going through. But how could I get prayer support from the congregation if they weren't allowed to know the truth? The Bible said that we ought to pray for one another, encourage one another, and build one another up. I had to find other friends to confide in.

Pretty soon though, Jeff stopped attending church altogether, and our usual second row seats were gradually given to others as Michelle and I were asked to sit a row farther back each Sunday. Eventually, we were seated in the back pew. I felt like a blemish that the pastor wanted to hide, the kind of blemish and canker sore that you cover up and push as far away from view as possible. I was a constant visual reminder of the ministry's failure to successfully restore a broken marriage. I felt that the pastor was embarrassed and ashamed of me. I took it personally. I felt betrayed and tossed aside, and I ended up leaving that church altogether.

With the plan to eventually reconcile, I revised my resume, answered a few want ads, and started pounding the pavement going on interviews. I registered my Pennsylvania protection from abuse order to Delaware, just in case.

I persuaded Jeff to file for Chapter 13 bankruptcy protection. He had gotten us into to serious debt by not paying the mortgage, truck note, and other bills. I was afraid of how our credit would be affected, but I plunged ahead anyway for our future benefit. The credit union called me to inform me that Jeff had overdrawn our account. I stayed on course and did not rescue him by paying the overdraft fees and replenishing the account. I simply allowed the account to be assessed the fees for him to reimburse. I no longer jumped in to save the day.

In June, we met with a bankruptcy attorney and officially filed for Chapter 13. Jeff was very skeptical dealing with lawyers and didn't feel our bankruptcy attorney deserved to be paid her fee, and Jeff often haggled with her. She was very patient with me but annoyed with Jeff's accusatory statements of mistrust. He resisted providing her with information she needed in order to represent us, so she routinely spoke only to me about getting the needed documents.

That wasn't the first time Jeff was rude and harsh with someone. He acted the same way with our mortgage broker when we were looking for a mortgage on the new house. I became the one the mortgage broker communicated with, since Jeff was so distrusting and suspicious. Sometimes Jeff would even accuse me of consorting with the "enemy" or having some type of non-professional relationship with people he did not get along with.

I faced another task on this road to reconciliation. I told my boss that I had decided to apply for the severance package the company was offering. I had worked there for over 13 years, and because of the problems Jeff had caused me on my job, it was time to leave. By that time, only a few coworkers knew that I had separated from my husband because of domestic violence and his drug abuse. I told my boss that I wanted to work on reconciliation and help my husband through a drug rehab program, but didn't know how to do it if I lived so far away. The severance package would be generous and would offer me a chance to walk away with a little nest egg and some cash to start my life over.

It was almost summer. I was focused on taking care of myself and I finally scheduled the foot surgery that the orthopedist recommended months ago. Since Michelle would be out on summer break, we could both stay at the house in Delaware while I recuperated. During that short stay, I found out that Jeff had been "entertaining" other women at the house in previous weeks. That's when I realized that reconciliation would not be an option. I was not going to tolerate his immoral behavior anymore, and, with this new ammunition, I packed up our things and returned to my apartment. This time it was for good.

***

Reflection:

A coworker cut out a Far Side comic strip and gave it to me one day at work. It depicted a group of seven mummies at a cocktail party with one animated woman mummy in the midst who wore glasses. She was smiling with a drink in her hand, captivating the others while telling a story. There were two women mummies in the foreground of the cartoon who were holding drinks, whispering and watching and saying:

"*Well, as usual, there goes Princess Luanna – always the center of attention. … You know, underneath that outer wrap, she's held together with duct tape.*

That cartoon reminded me of me. At times, I felt as though I was being held together with duct tape.

10
Feeling the Fear

*"For God hath not given us the spirit of fear; but of power,
and of love, and of a sound mind." – 2 Timothy 1:7*

Jeff called me at work and said that it was urgent that I see him. He said that he was very sick and needed to go to the doctor. He said that he could be dying. He asked me to go to the doctor's office with him. I said yes, took off from work that afternoon, and met him at my apartment. In the car on the way to the city, I asked him what was wrong. He said that something was terribly wrong and that he was afraid. I asked again what was wrong. He said he had a rash. I asked what kind of rash as I scanned his face, neck and hands. I didn't see anything from where I was sitting, and I reached for his shirt-tail and pulled it up. He had a rash all right. I suggested that maybe he was allergic to something he ate. I quizzed him about his diet, and he mentioned that it wasn't a food allergy. I wondered what on earth he could be talking about. He went back and forth with me throwing out possibilities, and he sheepishly replied that he didn't know what it was or what it could be. His answers were vague, and he kept telling me that he could be dying. He was really playing on my sympathies.

Then it dawned on me. He was playing a mind game with me. By now, we were in a familiar neighborhood of the city which was down the street from a public clinic. A clinic? I have insurance for the family, and we had our own doctors.

Why were we going into the city to a clinic? As we pulled into a parking spot in front of an office building, I realized that we had just arrived at a health clinic. The community clinic treated venereal diseases. I was stunned and silent. Once inside, I didn't say a word and followed Jeff's lead in anonymously filling out forms that lay in a basket on the counter. A woman sat behind a counter shielded by a bullet-proof Plexiglas window. She took my completed form in exchange for a numbered ticket. I sat down beside Jeff and wondered if I had syphilis, too.

As I waited, I watched others come in and fill out paperwork. There were about five or six men, but no women. It was in the middle of the afternoon so the men had either taken off from work, worked a late shift, or didn't have a job. One man appeared to know the routine and wasn't ashamed. He talked out loud about being there again. He joked and laughed with the receptionist and other men in the waiting room. A few were quiet and probably just as embarrassed as I was about being there. One man just sat there with a blank stare not making eye contact with anyone, trying to look calm and nonchalant but inwardly screaming with rage and anger about the woman who may have infected him. I wondered if any of the men thought I was the sister or friend of the man I was sitting next to. Maybe they thought I was there to give moral support and encouragement to my brother, cousin, or friend who didn't have anyone else to turn to for help. I had hoped that that was what they thought. But deep down inside, I suspected that they knew that one of us had given the other a sexually-transmitted disease. Maybe they thought that Jeff and I wanted to come clean and come together for medical attention as an act of repentant love. Or maybe they thought I was just plain stupid for being with a man who had cheated on me. Why did I worry about what these other men thought? I could not understand why it mattered to me at all.

A door opened, and the nurse called my number. I followed her and sat where directed. After telling her the reason for my visit, I was given literature about STDs and ushered into an examining room to be seen by a doctor. I was asked basic health and sexual history questions. My blood pressure, pulse, and temperature were taken. Blood was drawn, and I was examined. The initial result of the STD test came back negative, but I was still instructed to take all of the medication anyway and given a follow-up appointment for the results of the HIV test. I was also given a generous supply of condoms. I vowed that day that Jeff would never touch me sexually again. And I meant it.

By the end of July, I had resolved to sever marital ties with Jeff. I also decided to look for a different church to attend -- a healthier one. The pastor's advice to reconcile had just kicked me in the face. Full force in the face, and it hit me hard. Real hard.

***

During the next few months, my sister and I became much closer. She listened and empathized with me as I finally opened up and shared the turmoil I was going through. She told me to call her any time to talk about my frustrations. We occasionally went to the movies and out to dinner. Sometimes I'd drive over to her house, and we would just sit, talk, eat, and drink coffee. She was very honest with me and offered a lot of support and encouragement. She reassured me that I would overcome this trial and come out on top. Her confidence in me propelled me to press on towards healing.

My sister, Michelle, for whom my daughter was named, came along with me to Annapolis, Maryland, to the wedding of my friend, Ken Braithwaite, a decorated U.S. Naval officer, who was also one of my supervisors at work. His wedding was a beautiful affair. The pomp and circumstance of a military wedding ceremony wasn't something I had ever experienced, and I was honored to be his guest and pleased to have my sister come along with me. That wedding gave me a sense of hope and belief that you can find true love. And Ken was truly a romantic in every sense of the word. He was a trusting soul, with an angelic face and twinkling eyes. The rigorous military training had not taken a toll on his humanity or humility. He was a gentleman and deserved to have a wife who mirrored his demeanor. And when I met Melissa, I knew she would honor and trust him just as he would her. She truly was one of the most caring and gracious women I had ever met. Being an eyewitness to their love and romanticism lifted my spirits and gave me hope that one day I, too, would find love.

Unfortunately, their wedding day was marred. The wedding guests and bridal party had said farewell to the bride and groom as they boarded a small yacht to sail around the harbor for a quick getaway. We continued celebrating after the reception at a local pub when news came that Princess Diana was killed in an auto accident in France. As we mourned with one of the bridegrooms who was a British Naval officer, we couldn't help but think that on every wedding anniversary Ken and Melissa would be reminded that it was the same day that the world lost a Princess. My sister and I would always remember that day as well.

Within a week, I experienced just the opposite of true love.

My sister and I had planned to go to a play on September 5, 1997, and as I prepared an overnight bag for little Michelle, Jeff showed up unexpectedly at the apartment and wanted to take our daughter for the weekend. He was on his way to take Jeff, Jr. to New Jersey for his weekend military reserve duty. I told Jeff that we had other plans and that he could not take Michelle that night. Jeff became agitated and started to move restlessly throughout the apartment pacing back and forth between the living room and kitchen area. He started clenching his teeth as if he were about to explode. Then all of a sudden he picked up a kitchen chair and smashed it against the table, shattering the chair into pieces. I hardly had time to react before my seven-year-old screamed. I yelled for her to run into the back bedroom and lock the door. She ran to the back of apartment and I could hear her crying. Jeff's eyes looked wild, and he frantically looked around the room for something else to pick up.

He picked up another chair and began banging it against the floor yelling, "Why, why, why, are you doing this?" As the splintered pieces of wood went flying around the room, I backed up against the kitchen wall. By that time, Jeff, Jr. was yelling at his father, who was totally oblivious to his son's attempts at intervention. Jeff's rage led him to the TV. As he picked up the 19" television, he raised it over his head and came towards me. My back was up against the wall, and I realized that I was about to be seriously injured or even die in a split second. This man was about to kill me. Almost as fast as my son jumped in front of me, his father turned a few degrees to the right and smashed the television against the kitchen floor. The sound was excruciating. He was completely out of control, and with the piercing sound of crashing glass, you could see the light bulb go off in his head, and he realized that something horrible was happening. It was as though he had come back to his senses. My son was standing in front of me, shielding me from his father with his arm outstretched as he was prepared to block the TV from hitting me.

Suddenly, there was pounding on my apartment door. Someone was banging and yelling from the other side. I noticed that there was blood coming from somewhere. It wasn't mine. It wasn't Jeff's. It was my son's blood. His hand was bleeding, and broken glass and pieces of compressed wood were everywhere. The elder Jeff ran out of the apartment as soon as he realized what had happened and his son darted out after him in a flash. My neighbor was on the other side of the door, and when the pair flew past her, she stepped in to see if Michelle and I were okay. Jeff, Jr. had run out to his father's truck just in time to reach inside and smear blood on his father's shirt as he sped off.

I heard my daughter crying and whimpering from my bedroom. I ran back to her and convinced her that it was all right to unlock the door. I told her that daddy was gone and that it was okay to open the door. My neighbor had already called the police. She was a nurse and had heard all the commotion going on over her head. My son had come back to the apartment with his friend, Chris, who had been waiting in Jeff's truck. He was going to go along for the ride to New Jersey but was told to get out when Jeff was on the run. My neighbor washed my son's hand and recommended that he go to the hospital for stitches. His finger was badly cut, but thankfully it wasn't serious enough to require surgery. I clutched Michelle tightly and calmed her down. Jeff, Jr., on the other hand, was fuming, hurt, and bewildered. He could not understand how his father could come so close to killing me. The police arrived and took photos and each of our statements. I was told to file for another protection from abuse order and was informed that the next step would be a hearing. The officer and my neighbor left.

I surveyed the damage to my apartment and swept aside broken pieces of wood and glass, and made a pathway to the door. It was getting late, and I had to get my son to the hospital and get to my sister's house in time to get to the play. I gathered Michelle's things, locked the door, and left my apartment. My son assured me that he would be okay at the hospital. His friend would wait with him and I planned to see him later on that night or the next day. I grabbed my purse and little girl and headed to Philadelphia as planned. No sense crying over spilled milk. Tomorrow's another day.

It wasn't until a few days later that we found out that Jeff was hiding out at his cousin's home in Philadelphia. The police report had been filed. Jeff was charged with assault, battery, and a couple of other misdemeanors, and a hearing date was set. A girlfriend and former coworker of mine came along with me, and she gave me the support I needed. It gave me great comfort knowing that I was not going through this alone. The district attorney asked if I wanted to have Jeff put in jail, and I told him that it was not necessary. I believed that Jeff was remorseful, and I didn't want him to lose his business nor strip Jeff of his way of supporting himself and his children. There was no need to take his dignity because he just snapped. The court ordered Jeff to pay restitution and replace the TV and kitchenette set. He was also ordered to take an anger management course and to get drug and alcohol abuse counseling. I asked for a protection from abuse order. My request for the protective order was filed and scheduled for a hearing at a later date.

***

I was sitting in the courthouse waiting room hoping no one would walk in and recognize me. A petite woman about my age came in and sat near me. Her name was Felicia. We exchanged morning pleasantries and since we were there for the same reason, it was easy to strike up a conversation to seal our mutual bond. We had just exchanged numbers when we were called and escorted to the court room. There was a court stenographer, a state trooper, and another court official milling around in the chamber. A call to rise came, and the judge entered the room. The tall middle-aged man sat at the bench and reviewed my petition and complaint, asked me a few questions to verify my statements, and without hesitation, granted me a protection from abuse order. I breathed a sigh of relief as though I was a convicted felon awaiting a death sentence who had instead been granted a full pardon. Funny how a victim can sometimes think that she is the criminal. Weird, huh?

The judge went through the same exercise with my newfound friend and granted her a protection from abuse order as well. We smiled an uneasy smile at each other and promised to talk later that night. Our friendship was sealed.

For the remainder of the year, I decided to look for another job near our apartment. It was apparent that I was never going back to Delaware. I also devoted a lot of my time to taking care of my daughter. I signed Michelle up for gymnastics classes on Saturday mornings and took her on special trips. At Christmas time, the two of us went to Washington, DC, and toured the White House, monuments, and museums.

My sister and I attended my childhood friend's wedding, where I served as a hostess. We also managed to squeeze in a day trip to Atlantic City with our cousin, and during the quiet Christmas holiday week, a few close girlfriends came to visit. They listened to me, encouraged me, and prayed with me. They even helped me reminisce about the good old days as we looked through photo albums and shared memories. That was a reflective time for me even though I filled up my calendar with activities and events. Attending to different events and functions kept my mind off of my troubles and worries, and helped me focus on and treasure my friends and family. It was indeed a healing period to be surrounded by those who loved me. I didn't feel isolated anymore.

***

Reflections:

1. Break the silence about abuse and tell somebody... anybody!
2. Press charges!
3. Protect yourself from sexually transmitted diseases and use condoms!

PART III
BUILDING A NEW LIFE

11
Friends

"People will forget what you said; people will forget what you did, but people will never forget how you made them feel." – Maya Angelou

"A man that hath friends must show himself friendly: and there is a friend that sticketh closer than a brother." – Proverbs 18:24

I started 1998 by redeeming a gift certificate for a full spa treatment. It was a wonderfully relaxing luxury that I couldn't afford on a regular basis, but I decided I would try to occasionally pamper myself. I thought it was time for me to start doing things for myself. That led me to accept the company's voluntary termination package. The severance package would give a needed lift to my almost non-existent savings account, allow me to purchase a car, take a couple of vacations, invest in mutual funds, and start a college fund for Michelle. I didn't know if Jeff would be willing to pay for Michelle's education let alone pay child support. The only thing I did know was that it was my responsibility to take care of my daughter. I could not depend on Jeff. He had made it quite clear that he would fight me in court if I ever went after him for child support.

I didn't just get some money in the New Year; I also got a new job. One of my coworkers, a patent attorney, recommended me to his friend who was the president of a hardware manufacturing company. His friend needed an assistant and wondered if I would be interested in applying. I didn't need to think about it long, and I accepted the invitation to talk to his friend. I met the President, but was not offered the job. Instead, I was asked to interview for and was offered a totally different job. I thought, "God really works in mysterious ways." As a learning center associate, I would schedule all training programs, register employees for online and group training sessions, and maintain training records, reports, and program materials for all U.S. employees. I accepted the offer.

The welcome I received on my very first day was more than I had ever expected. The staff treated me like a skilled professional who would make a great impact in the training department. The work was rewarding, and I was well respected. Coworkers valued my opinion, and my recommendations and suggestions were implemented. My confidence began to build, and I started to feel significant.

In a short period of time, I began to trust my instincts again. I was confident in my decision-making and thought processes and wasn't second-guessing myself. However, I was still unsure of myself in my personal affairs. I didn't possess that same sense of confidence and was indecisive about working things out with Jeff. So, I decided not to decide. I didn't want to think about him or the marriage and focused only on building a new career and on caring for my daughter.

Michelle seemed to be adjusting well to her new school and surroundings, and I felt that our lives had reached a level of normalcy and routine. She participated in Saturday morning gymnastics and made new friends in the apartment complex. I even met a few of the neighbors. Michelle seemed delighted and content with her friends, and she enjoyed playing with them. I was convinced that if I focused on her happiness, I would be happy.

We had a roof over our heads, a nice apartment, basic provisions, transportation, and I had a job I enjoyed. Yet, I still felt empty and lifeless. I knew that my faith and trust in God had guided me to that point, but I couldn't put my finger on why I felt so lost. That's when I realized that I missed Jeff. I missed having him cook, clean, and run our household. I missed having the security of his protection. I missed his loud and boisterous declarations of strength and confidence, which gave me a sense of reassurance. I missed being held in his arms, nuzzling my face in his chest, and smelling him. I couldn't stop thinking about him.

I wasn't sleeping well. I was waking up in the middle of the night with a sense of fear and dread and couldn't get back to sleep. I worried about all kinds of things that could go wrong. What if something would happen to Michelle while I was at work, and I couldn't get to her in time? What if I got into an accident and no one knew about it? What if the auto mechanic overcharged me for brake work or the transmission blew? Or what if no one was around to take care of Michelle because Jeff was missing in action on one of his drug or alcohol binges and couldn't be found? What if someone broke into the apartment and robbed us, or worse yet, raped or killed us? I couldn't sleep thinking about the horrible things that could befall us.

I really missed Jeff. But, I had left him, and now it was my responsibility to protect our daughter. I had given up my right to be protected by a husband. I was both the mother and father now. I would be the one who had to make sure that someone would pick up Michelle from school if I had to work late. I would be the one who had to learn more about cars and repairs and make sure I wasn't getting ripped off by the mechanic. I would be the one who had to make sure the apartment door was bolted and locked and that the patio door had the block in place so an intruder couldn't slide the door open.

I felt overwhelmed with all this responsibility, and for a little while, I regretted leaving Jeff. No wonder I couldn't go to sleep after all my worrying. And when I did fall asleep it was time to get up. I would be exhausted at work. A coworker recommended drinking a cup of warm milk whenever I had these bouts of sleeplessness and I found that it really helped -- for a little while, anyway. When I finally complained to my doctor, she prescribed medication to help me sleep at night and to help ease my anxiety.

During one of my sessions with Larry, I told him that:

1. I felt no control over my life;
2. I was disappointed, down, and depressed;
3. I did not want reconciliation; and
4. I could not get up or get motivated.

I spent most of the time in his office blowing my nose, whimpering, and wiping away uncontrollable tears as I recounted how painful it was being married and being alone at the same time. I felt that I was a failure and that no one understood how complicated it was to love the person who had beaten the living crap out of you. I dreaded being the kind of woman who deserved no pity for putting up with abuse. Larry said that my feelings were normal and recommended that I start doing things that I liked and not be afraid to venture out and to try new things. He warned me that just staying at home and wrapping my life around Michelle was not healthy. After that session, I went back to my apartment totally exhausted with swollen, bleary, red eyes and went to bed without eating…again. I had gotten used to hunger pangs and ignored my belly's cry for food.

***

I sat on the floor with the remote in my hand flicking through the channels on TV and skimming through the Sunday paper. I didn't go to church that day. It didn't matter. Nobody would know or care that I didn't show up. Nobody missed me and I didn't want to see anybody anyway. A commercial came on advertising cruises. I remembered what Larry said about doing things that I liked and that commercial sparked my interest. I searched the paper for the travel and leisure section. There were a lot of sales in the newspaper, and since I had a little extra cash I considered the possibility of taking a trip. I called my sister and asked if she'd be interested in going on an inexpensive cruise with me, and she agreed. The excitement of getting away to a tropical island gave me a little rush. I felt liberated, and it felt good. I began to think about what I would buy to wear for the trip. I thought it would be fun to pick out new swim suits and cute little shorts and tops, especially since I had lost over 20 pounds. I booked our flights and off we went to board a cruise ship docked in Miami, Florida, and bound for the Bahamas.

My sister and I had a wonderful time on our mini-vacation. We made new friends, and I became the object of affection for one of the crew members. It seems silly now, but at the time, being pursued by such a handsome man really boosted my ego. I enjoyed the attention so much that I booked a second trip within six weeks. After the second trip, however, I realized that I was making a fool of myself and being quite ridiculous. It was very silly to think that lasting happiness could ever be found during a vacation to a tropical island. Things like that only happen in movies like *How Stella Got Her Groove Back*. Come to think of it, even though the movie was based on true life, we all know what happened afterwards. It didn't last.

After the cruise, I started doing things to pamper myself, including regularly-scheduled hair salon appointments. It seemed like a small start, but at least it was one. Slowly but surely, I began taking short day or weekend trips and ventured out to develop the new friendships I had made in the past couple of months. I kept in touch with some of the women I met during the cruises and made plans to visit them.

I also started going regularly to a new church. I met the pastor, who recommended I sign up and attend the new members' class to learn more about the church and to meet others. I also had a short meeting with him to explain my situation. He was very encouraging and suggested that I continue on my course of getting counseling with a mental health professional. I met a few members of the church and was introduced to a gentleman who had inquired about me. I was polite during the introduction and after a few weeks I agreed to have lunch with him. We talked about the cultural mix of the congregation, our mutual friends, and our marital situations -- his being divorced and my being separated. He recommended the law firm he used to get his divorce and explained that the cost would be around $300 and that everything would be done through the mail. He expressed an interest in seeing more of me. I was not interested in seeing him. Instead, I told him that I wasn't ready for anything more than just a friendship. I have heard it said that things happen for a reason and that God places certain people in our lives for a particular purpose. It might be for a very short season and just for one reason. I believed that this man was hand-picked by God to come into my life just for that purpose. I knew that it was meant for me to have his divorce attorney's phone number.

***

My courtroom buddy, Felicia and I wanted to celebrate our new lives apart from our abusers, so we made reservations at a very upscale Delaware restaurant with live R&B music. We treated ourselves to a delicious dinner in the main dining room, and were seated by a window with a lovely view of the river. It felt good being surrounded by beautiful, successful people. After dinner, we went to listen to the band, where it was standing room only. We stood near the bar waiting for two stools to open up. A beautiful, tall, silver-haired middle-aged woman sitting at the bar motioned to me and asked if we wanted the seats her parents were vacating. I thanked her, and as her parents left, we took the seats next to her.

She started a conversation and asked what had brought me to the restaurant. I explained that my friend and I were celebrating our emancipation from our abusive spouses, and she began to tell me about the loss of her love, who had died recently. Her name was Marjorie English, and by the end of the night she had declared herself to be my adopted big sister. She would help me regain my self esteem and would teach me how to recognize healthy relationships. Little did I know that Marjorie would be a good friend for a very long time. Even longer than my courtroom buddy, Felicia.

Marjorie invited me to be her guest at a networking conference the following week. I had never been to a professional networking event before and I eagerly accepted her invitation. It was the second annual convention sponsored by a major oil company for its African-American employees throughout the country. The program included various workshops, from balancing work and family life and strengthening communication skills, to team-building and professional development. I eagerly attended every session of interest. I even persuaded my boss to give me time off from work to attend. He not only allowed me to participate during work hours; he also paid for all incidental expenses I incurred and applied the hours to my training profile. During the conference, I met some wonderful people who would help me get through some of the most difficult times yet to come.

12
In Therapy

"Happy is the man that findeth wisdom, and the man that getteth understanding:" – Proverbs 3:13

It was August, and I was feeling strong and optimistic. With this newfound strength, I was able to make some powerful and profound moves toward healing. I called the divorce attorney that my friend from church had recommended. A few days later, I received a packet containing a letter outlining court procedures, filing fees, timeline, forms, and a questionnaire. I mulled it over for a day or so before filling out the questionnaire to start the process.

Jeff became very agitated when I told him about my decision to file for a divorce. He would call me at work several times a day and would yell at me about breaking up the family. I was tempted to call the police and report the harassing phone calls, but I called Jeff's defense attorney instead and told him that I filed for divorce and asked him to remind his client of the standing court order of protection. I was taking advantage of this new surge of strength and empowerment and was not going to put up with Jeff's intimidation and threats anymore. The calls stopped.

Within a week or so, I felt good enough to drive 600 miles to visit a girlfriend whom I had met during the cruise. She lived in Norfolk, Virginia, and had invited me and my daughter down for the weekend. It was one of the most challenging things I had ever done. To get into a car with a child and drive that distance alone would have been quite scary for me a year before, but things were starting to look up.

After the trip, I invited another girlfriend from the cruise to travel from Pawtucket, Rhode Island, to visit with us. Sharlene had become a good friend since we met on the cruise, and there was a deep sense of sisterhood between us. She was recently divorced. During her visit, we took our daughters on day trips to an amusement park, the zoo, and other fun places, and one night I asked my oldest daughter Christine to babysit the girls so Sharlene and I could go out to dinner, meet some of my friends, and dance the night away. We enjoyed each others' company, and she understood what I was going through. She was glad that I had started the divorce proceedings and was happy that something positive was happening for me.

***

I met some interesting people during the networking conference and a few of the men were calling now for dates. I was flattered but very cautious and leery about going out with them. I watched carefully for clues of aggression or suppressed anger in each of them. During dates, I would fish around and pose questions about previous relationships, and asked what they would do if women provoked them to such uncontrollable anger that they would want to hit them. I tried to make my inquiries subtly, however I was sure that some of my dates suspected that I was psychologically damaged from being abused. I was probably paranoid about that, too. One might even have thought that my view of all men was tainted by my husband. I tried to find the slightest flaw or weakness in a man's character to justify my immediate dash from the scene.

However, their responses were all pretty much the same. None admitted that they had experienced violence in any previous relationship. Not one admitted to succumbing to fits of rage when provoked by a woman. I wondered why and pondered this new breed of man that I had not been exposed to in my forty years on this planet. Was it because these men all had rewarding jobs and were successful? I had quit college after only one semester and married young, so I never had a chance to come across college-educated African-American men. They were rare in the workplace. My father and husband never attended college, and my brother, Donnie, dropped out of college under extreme mental stress. Unfortunately, I didn't grow up around successful men and didn't have any male role models to look up to. I wasn't used to being around intelligent level-headed men with prosperous careers.

***

Also, during this time of strength, I began to open up and talk more to Larry about what was bothering me. No doubt the medication I was taking had something to do with this new sense of optimism. I was able to see and think a lot more clearly now. I had listed all of the blessings and all the things that I was grateful for in my life, and I was also able to clearly identify the source of the anger and rage I had inside. There were a lot of people I was angry with. I was angry with my mother, my brother, my youngest sister, my husband, his family, and even some of my husband's so-called friends. It was his friends who didn't have the courage to confront him about his misdeeds, philandering, and drug use. Not one of them held him accountable for hitting me. Not one of them stood up for me. I guess they were afraid of Jeff as much as I was.

During one session, I complained that even some of Jeff's own siblings harbored him during his binges. The nerve! The gall! I was the one who kept their brother afloat all those years while he dibbled and dabbled in this and that trying to find himself. I was the one who kept a steady job. I was the one who helped him build his business and his dream house. I was the one. I recalled how some of them wouldn't even help me when I told them that he was kicking my butt, stealing from the family, cheating on me, and using crack cocaine. I knew some of them never liked me anyway.

One of Jeff's siblings told him that I was too black and asked Jeff why he was marrying me in the first place. While sitting in Larry's office, I began to cry out loud asking myself why I had married into that family and threatened that I was going to tell all of their dirty little secrets to the world. I felt hurt and betrayed. Have you ever been so angry that you could spit bullets? Have you ever wanted to spew all kinds of derogatory filthy language you could think of and hurl it against your enemies, but when it was all over, you were embarrassed that you had let yourself yield to such immaturity? Well, that was how I felt during one session with Larry as I released all the pain that was pent up inside of me. I was mad as hell and angry about being alone and having to do everything by myself with no one to help me. I asked myself, "After all I had done for Jeff out of love, what did I have to show for it?" Nothing. Not a doggone thing. I was angry at Jeff for putting me in this predicament. I asked the Lord, "Why?"

All I ever wanted was to be safe from the cruelty of the world and to be loved in all my blackness. I wanted to be with someone who loved me just as I was. And I was really pissed off. I felt like I got the short end of the stick. I got punched in the face, spit upon, kicked, choked, raped, slapped, and all sorts of things that no one ever deserved. He once even pulled me off the toilet and smashed food in my face and in my hair. He threw things at me and left bruises that I hid from the world. I was now able to express my anger clearly in counseling. I was finally able to write down and speak about all the good, the bad, and the ugly. And, believe me, the ugly was real ugly.

Larry listened and was very patient, empathetic, and caring as new revelations started coming out of me. I knew, however, that it would soon be time to say goodbye to my marriage counselor. I had initially started seeing Larry as a family and marriage counselor, with the intent of reconciling with Jeff. But now it wasn't going to be necessary. There was no marriage to put back together. In a few months, I wouldn't need his services anymore since I had decided to end the marriage. But I wasn't quite ready to sever ties with my counselor. I still had some kinks to work out.

***

Over the next couple of months and through the end of the year, my social life became more active. I continued to pamper myself with regular hair appointments, listening to my favorite gospel music, and even starting massage therapy. A friend of mine from my former church had started her own business as a masseuse, and I had become a regular customer. She would come to my apartment with her table, candles, and soothing music and would treat my stressed-out body to a 30-minute massage. As she worked out the kinks and knots in my shoulders, neck, and back, we had calming conversations about things I could do to better care for myself.

Another treat was taking walks during lunch with a Christian coworker named Tiffany. Most times I would have only half a sandwich and a small drink at lunchtime, and afterwards, Tiffany and I would talk about all the good things that the Lord was doing in our lives. The daily ritual helped clear my head and helped me realize that God was still in control of my life and that He would work things out for my good. The Bible says in Romans 8:28, "And we know that all things work together for good to them that love God, to them who are the called according to his purpose." I was constantly reminded of His goodness, compassion, and loving kindness, and this truly inspired me to continue with my Christian walk no matter what challenge I was facing. Now if only I could eat more than just half a sandwich.

I was walking through the cafeteria one day on my way to the mailroom and noticed the company's facility manager sitting at one of the tables meeting with someone. I looked at the other man and recognized him instantly. I stopped in my tracks and turned to greet my former boss, Fred Carpenter.

Remember I said that God puts people in your life for a reason and some only for a season? Well, this was one of those times. I hadn't seen Fred since I left the engineering company in the city back in 1985 over 13 years ago. After his meeting with Don, we went to lunch at a local café. He had come to our company to sell his engineering consulting capabilities and to get leads on projects. Don was interested in contracting with Fred's company and would be in contact with him in the near future.

In the meantime, Fred and I had a lot of catching up to do. His wife had died from cancer a few years earlier and their kids were all grown now. I told him about what was going on with me and we agreed to talk later. Fred recalled how possessive Jeff was and suspected that he wasn't such a nice person. I recalled how much I had learned from him while working together years ago, and how much I missed his quick-witted humor. Our friendship was rekindled, and even though he was 20 years older than I was, there was a special connection between us.

We enjoyed long telephone conversations, and he was always long-winded, with many stories and adventures in his repertoire. Salesmen have that knack of captivating an audience. And he captivated me. He was going through a bout of depression himself since losing his wife, and we listened to each other, so I wasn't surprised when he asked me out for dinner. Then another. And another. I would tease him about how unlikely a pair we were, with him being a middle-aged white man wining and dining a younger black woman. I would make him laugh and blush as I held on to his hand or grabbed his arm as we walked down quaint little streets in the heart of the city to some expensive restaurant. We were amused by the stares and thought how silly it was for people to judge others by the color of their skin.

We talked about how we could boost one another up and we cheered each others' accomplishments. When he was down,

I lifted him up, and when I was down he cheered me on. I was fortunate to have someone like Fred as a friend. He affirmed me and assured me that nothing was wrong with me and that I had a lot to offer. He said any man would be happy to have me. He recommended that I join a local African-American ski club to keep myself busy and active. It was these kinds of suggestions and comments that helped build my confidence as well as deepen our friendship. He taught me a whole lot more in my later years than when I worked for him as his secretary. And I still enjoy his friendship many years later.

***

A friend of mine named Jerry and I sat in his car in my apartment complex parking lot one night. We had just returned from attending a restaurant food show at one of the airport hotels. As we sat, a car crossed in front of us, and I glanced over and saw the driver's profile. My heart skipped a beat. Then it started to beat wildly as if to burst through my chest as I watched the man peer into the darkness of the parking lot as if he were searching for someone. I reached for Jerry's arm and told him that the driver of the car was Jeff. I was frightened, and pointed in the direction of the passing car. Jerry saw the fear on my face, started the engine, and pulled out of the parking spot. He told me to breathe slowly and to calm down and asked me where the nearest police station was. Jeff saw us pulling out of the parking spot, turned his car around, and followed behind as we made the left turn out of the lot onto the main street.

Jerry was a police officer and immediately reminded me of a very valuable lesson about safety. He said that I should always park my car with the front facing out so I could easily make a quick getaway whenever threatened, or if ever I had to leave in a hurry. Jerry drove slowly and carefully down the hill, and as I peered into the passenger side mirror, I could see that Jeff was still following us. All I could think of was the rage that Jeff was probably feeling at seeing me with another man.

I was breathing hard and fast and couldn't slow my racing heart. Jerry continued to reassure me that everything would be okay and that I would be safe. When we were within a block of the police station, suddenly Jeff made a sharp left turn off the street. We continued to the station and pulled into the parking lot. Jeff was not behind us. Jerry got out and rang the bell since the main door of the station was locked. I locked the car doors. A police officer answered the door and came out. Jerry flashed his shield and explained my plight. The officer followed us back to my apartment where I made a statement about the stalking incident.

After the babysitter, Jerry, and the police officer left, I prepared for bed and the phone rang. It was Jeff complaining that I had left Michelle with some stranger while I was out with some dude. He yelled at me and accused me of being irresponsible. I told him that he was not to be near me or at the apartment and that I had filed a police report. Then, I hung up on him. He called back, apologized, and said that he wouldn't bother me anymore. He had been saying that for weeks now.

Ever since I told him that I wanted a divorce, he had been agreeable to whatever terms and conditions I wanted. He said he would do anything so I wouldn't take Michelle away from him. I believed he was truly sorry about the disintegration of our marriage. He had agreed to take responsibility for making the monthly Chapter 13 payments as long as I would not pursue him for child support. He said I could have anything I wanted from the house. He had planned to move back to Philadelphia. We made arrangements to move some furniture into storage, and other things to my apartment. I reminded Jeff that stalking me was not a wise move and was grounds for additional legal action that I was sure he did not want to experience. Again, he apologized, said he wouldn't bother me anymore, and hung up the phone with the same sound of despair and resignation that I had become accustomed to. But I knew he would call again. He always did.

I called Jerry and thanked him for helping me that evening. I hoped that Jeff hadn't scared him away. Jerry said that he wasn't intimidated by Jeff, and that he could've taken care of him in the parking lot. But that would not have been wise. I suspected that the stalking incident didn't play in my favor, and its negative impact hurt my chances of having a meaningful relationship with any man. I would always wonder if Jeff would be lurking around the next corner or pose a threat to me. I felt the need to protect Jerry. I knew how violent Jeff could get and was afraid that Jeff might snap and possibly injure or kill somebody in a fit of rage.

A few days later, all that anxiety and worry about having to look over my shoulder hit me full force. I started to panic and called Larry. I needed to know why I was so scared and wanted to know what was triggering these feelings. When I finally got a hold of him he recommended that I just relax and trust my gut. I determined that the real problem was that I had baggage that I was carrying around and that it could affect romantic relationships, so I decided not to get serious about anyone for the time being.

I did, however, enjoy juggling my schedule to accommodate dates as often as twice a week. I was having fun and always prefaced my dates with the "I'm a Christian going through a divorce and just want to be friends" line. It worked for a while, but whenever things got sticky (as it was only a matter of time before they hinted at wanting more than a platonic relationship) I would gently ease back and become unavailable for future dates. Maybe it wasn't fair to them, but I needed to protect my fragile heart and not dump my baggage into anyone else's yard. I needed to protect myself. Most of the gentlemen seemed to understand that and allowed me to graciously bow out of the dance.

I continued taking the medications and kept the regularly-scheduled doctor appointments to monitor my progress. I was sleeping a little better and could concentrate on things that needed to be done. At Thanksgiving, Michelle and I traveled to Pawtucket, Rhode Island to visit Sharlene and her family. It was the first time I hadn't cooked Thanksgiving dinner in a long time, and it was good being surrounded by friends who accepted me just as I was.

I wanted to continue getting positive feedback and assurances from good experiences, and I decided to change my memories and get rid of the garbage in my life. I decided to keep the good stuff and throw out the bad. People die and people leave us. People come in and out of our lives and relationships change. I had wanted Jeff to truly love me, protect me, and take care of me. I had wanted to be happily married all my life, but that changed. I needed to accept that. But one truth stayed with me – that even if people and relationships change – Jesus Christ will never change! The Bible says in Hebrews 13:8, "Jesus Christ the same yesterday, and to day, and for ever."

***

On December 12, 1998, I had my last marriage counseling session with Larry. Those final kinks related to my marriage dissolved and our working relationship was over.

I decided that it was time for me to work on understanding myself and to learn how my childhood and married life would affect me after the divorce. And, on my first appointment with Pat Lavin, a clinical social worker, she explained that the sense of loss I was experiencing was normal and that with time the pain of the divorce would ease. She recommended that I continue doing things that I enjoyed but to be careful not to overdo it. She said that I needed to reflect on the good things in my life and realize that the worst was behind me.

Just before Christmas, Jeff asked to borrow $100, and I gave it to him. No questions. I didn't care what he needed it for. I just wanted to be done with him and for him to leave me alone. In actuality, I guess I still needed to be needed by him -- to be his caretaker and to continue in my familiar and comfortable role of codependency. The need to be connected to him after all the hurt and pain he had caused our family had to end. I needed to stop taking care of him. I knew what I had to do, but couldn't seem to step off the merry-go-round. I took a hot air balloon ride the day after Christmas and while floating along in the cold, blue sky, I couldn't help wondering about how glorious this place called Earth is. I thought about how God created beauty everywhere, and I realized that He created beauty in me, too. I reflected on this and wished I could just float away from all my troubles. But I knew I had to face the music. I needed to step out of the basket, to get off of the merry-go-round, and start walking around among the living.

A few days later, I received the officially stamped and filed divorce decree in the mail. It was final. I got what I wanted but wondered why I felt so empty. There would be no reconciliation with Jeff. There would be no going back. There would be no spiritual covering over me. No man to protect me. No man to pray for me. No man to provide and care for me. There would be no one to stand up for me, and I felt quite alone and vulnerable in this big, open space. I was feeling very sorry for myself and continued to lament. True, I was officially divorced and free to marry again, but I wasn't jumping up and down, singing, and dancing. I should've felt like a heavy weight was lifted off of my shoulders. Instead, I felt a deep sense of loss. For 23 years, I had made it my life's mission to love, honor, cherish, and obey (yes, obey) one man until death do us part. And I loved him very much. My purpose was to be his helpmeet, and I had been a really good one. But, now I was a statistic. I felt like I was a failure and that people would look at me and wonder why I wasn't married. I believed that people would wonder what I had done to make him want to divorce me and what dirty little secret made me unfit. What was wrong with me? These thoughts overtook me and I began to doubt myself.

I thought, surely, we could have worked things out and reconciled. I began to believe that somehow I had failed at looking for all possible options for fixing the marriage. I had heard that a Christian couple got back together and remarried each other after divorce, and thought that this could be a possibility for us. All Jeff had to do was get his act together. He would have to stop drinking alcohol. He would have to stop using crack cocaine. He would have to stop cheating on me. He must stop hitting me. He must go to counseling for anger management, alcohol and drug abuse treatment, etc., etc., etc. I would have to learn how not to antagonize him. I would have to learn how to lift him up and to encourage him to be the best he could be. I would have to learn how to always be cheerful and pleasant and…I must…be out of my mind! This man almost killed me. And he almost killed me more than once. Snap out of it, girl! Get yourself together! But I couldn't get myself together. I needed to step off of the merry-go-round. I needed some help.

***

Reflections:
1. Learn how to protect yourself against a stalker.
2. Individual counseling, therapy, and support groups for domestic abuse survivors can help you process what you've been through and help you learn how to build new and healthy relationships with people.

13
A New Direction

"When you get to the end of all the light you know and it's time to step into the darkness of the unknown, faith is knowing that one of two things shall happen: either you will be given something solid to stand on, or you will be taught how to fly." – Edward Teller

"What the caterpillar calls the end of the world, the master calls a butterfly." – Richard Bach

It was February 1999, and I had been feeling really gloomy. I just thought that I was going through a rough patch and would bounce back in a little while. My doctor told me I was suffering from clinical depression with codependent tendencies. She increased the dosage of the antidepressant I had been taking to help me sleep and told me to continue to see the clinical social worker. Since I had lost some weight, she also told me to keep a journal and to keep track of the food I ate. She said I was in a critically vulnerable state and would start feeling worse as the reality of being divorced set in.

When I got home from the doctor's office, I received a call from Darryl, a friend of the family, who told me that Jeff was missing. I started to panic and wondered what awful thing could have happened to him. I thought that Jeff was probably upset about the divorce and might want to kill himself. Or maybe he had overdosed on drugs and was lying dead in some back alley. I regained my composure and recognized the increased anxiety that was beginning to well up in me. I breathed deeply and slowly and with clarity told our friend that I didn't know where Jeff was and that he should try calling him again in a few days. I reassured him that Jeff would turn up whenever he was ready to be found and gently and politely ended the call. I inwardly rejoiced that I overcame the urge to join in the search and rescue for Jeff. It felt good not to jump into my superwoman suit to save the day.

I followed my doctor's advice and began keeping track of my meals. The log showed me that I wasn't eating much at all. I would skip breakfast, eat half a sandwich and walk a little during lunch, and go straight to bed when I got home. With this new information about my eating pattern I was able to make a conscious effort to improve my health by eating three meals a day. I had to purposely eat breakfast and make sure I ate a full sandwich at lunchtime. But most evenings I would only eat a light dinner, if any at all. This exercise was a step in the right direction to regain my strength and weight.

My attempts to make Michelle's life more interesting and fun to make up for not having her dad around didn't work out as well as I had hoped. I was missing Jeff terribly and couldn't understand why. I didn't want my misery to rub off on her, so I planned sleepovers, play dates, and activities to keep her occupied.

I forced myself to accept invitations to parties, events, and galas with my new friends and made plans to stay busy to avert a deeper state of depression as I tried to refute the diagnosis. I pulled myself together to go to a gospel concert with my sister, Michelle, and I attended my company's annual semi-formal dinner party.

During the dinner party, one of my coworkers named Dwayne urged to me to go on a weekend Vermont ski excursion that his club was sponsoring. He persisted until I surrendered and signed up for the trip. During the pajama party event, I felt like I was on a safari in Africa. The event reminded me of the movie *How Stella Got Her Groove Back* when Angela Bassett went to the pajama beach party with Whoopi Goldberg and saw that most attendees were scantily dressed. In the movie, women were walking around half naked and the men were on the prowl wearing only Speedos or thongs. I felt extremely out of place on the trip and my uneasiness showed. I mentioned to Dwayne that this type of event was not my kind of fun. He said that he knew I would feel awkward but would at least be out of the house and would have a good laugh.

Another activity of the weekend was a trip to the town's roller skating rink. Now this activity was something I could enjoy. It reminded me of my teenage years in the 70's when we wore big Afros, hooped earrings, polyester print shirts, halter tops, and bell-bottomed hipster jeans. As a teenager, I remembered coming home after a night of skating with friends with a coating of white dust in our hair and wondering where it had come from, not realizing that we had skated so much that we had scraped up the wood-planked floors from the rink. Those were the good old days. And if you ever saw the movie *Roll Bounce* that was released in the movie theaters in 2005, you'd know what I was talking about.

After thinking about this whole outing, I really did appreciate Dwayne for coaxing me to experience something I would not have normally ventured out to do. I guess he saw the stress I was under and wanted to cheer me up. I forgave him, but at the end of the trip, I told him not to ever invite me to anything like that again. And, after all that, I didn't even get a chance to ski.

After that experience, I didn't venture out again for several months.

***

It was early one Saturday morning in April, and I just couldn't get out of bed. It was windy and chilly, and the trees were still bare. I pulled the covers up around my neck and snuggled in against my pillow. I could hear the familiar sounds of cartoons coming from the living room and knew that Michelle was up already. I hoped that she had eaten a bowl of cereal. It was just too early, I thought, and I didn't want to face another day. But it wasn't early at all. It was near noon.

The phone rang, and the woman on the line asked if I owned the house on Cornwell Drive. I was afraid it was a collection agency, a bank, or the mortgage company trying to track me to make a payment. It had been a few months now, and I knew that Jeff wasn't making them. Maybe the lender wanted to foreclose on the house. But it was Saturday morning. What business establishment would call someone on the weekend? They must be desperate. I was nervous as I confirmed my identity and ownership of the house. You could hear the sigh of relief in the caller's voice. She introduced herself and explained that she had been searching for me. She had asked some of the neighbors on the street how to contact me, because she and her husband wanted to buy the house. I was in a state of shock. I sat up in bed. My mood lightened, and you could hear the excitement in my voice. I was relieved to get such a pleasant call on that chilly Saturday in April.

After we made plans to talk early the next week, I hung up the phone and jumped up out of bed. I danced a little dance, shouted a little shout, and thanked the Lord for getting us out from under the heavy burden of owning a home that we were not living in. In the weeks to come, Jeff would agree to their offer. We sold the house in a short sale and had no further financial obligation to the property.

***

Within a few weeks, I was feeling better and attributed my optimism to three important people in my life -- my sister, Michelle, and two close friends, named Rhoda and Linette. They gave me a lot of emotional support and helped to rebuild my self-esteem. They encouraged me to get out and do new things. I had known Rhoda since elementary school. We had become even closer when I finally told her about the domestic abuse I was going through. She was very upset that I had never, in the slightest way, mentioned the problems I was having. I explained to her that my silence was a part of the symptoms of domestic violence. Women are ashamed and embarrassed about it and do not tell. That's what kept the cycle going -- secrecy. Rhoda was also brutally honest with me about my weight loss and kept me motivated to get healthy. I knew she would tell me the truth even if it hurt my pride. Rhoda loved me and helped me adjust to single life as we planned to do things together. In May, she invited me to go on vacation with her to the Bahamas.

I had known Linette and her family since 1983. I remember when she provided comfort when Jeff cheated on me while I was pregnant with Michelle. It was Linette who helped me realize that I wasn't the one with the problem and that I should not blame myself for my husband's actions. But, it was Linette's husband, Reggie, who confronted me with the possibility that I was appeasing Jeff and that I could have codependent tendencies. I didn't know it at the time, but he was right. I went along with the game just to avoid a fight. I know now that that was not the best course of action. I really appreciated Linette and Reggie and what they did for me. Linette was always there to listen to me whenever I called her and she constantly called to check up on me to make sure I was doing okay. Her unconditional love for me kept me going.

Over the next few months, I enjoyed a reunion with my friends from the networking conference and went to Charlotte, North Carolina. In August, I did double duty and went solo on a five-day trip to London, and upon my return home, I went skydiving after being inspired by a coworker to take the plunge. In September, I took Michelle to Niagara Falls with my girlfriend Barbara and her mentee from the Big Brothers and Big Sisters organization. It was a busy summer, and it felt good to be alive. I was traveling and doing all kinds of things to lift my spirits. I wanted to experience life to its fullest, but little did I know that another adventure was just around the bend.

***

I was following up on some leads to build a long distance telephone service company for a friend and called my former boss Jyrl Ann James. She told me that she was moving back to the east coast because her company was moving its headquarters to New York. I told her I was excited about getting the chance to see her and the kids again once she got settled and asked her to call me if she needed anything. A few days later she called me back and asked if I would consider moving to be her executive assistant. She said that I was the best secretary she had ever had and would love for us to work together again. I hesitated and reminded her that it was pretty expensive to make such a move to New York and that I couldn't afford it. She said that she would make the job and the experience worthwhile.

Within a couple of weeks, I was headed to the Long Island office to meet with Jyrl and the Legal department staff, and to tour the surrounding area with a real estate broker to look for a place to live. A few days after that visit, I received a formal offer that included a significant increase in my salary, a sign-on bonus, a moving package, and, more importantly, a life insurance benefit that paid well. I was thinking about providing for my children in the event something were to happen to me. I was ecstatic and accepted the offer.

This was going to be an opportunity of a lifetime, and I wasn't about to pass it up. I promised myself that I would try new things to expand my horizons. I promised myself that I would take on challenges that forced me to come out of my comfort zone and to stretch my mind and faith. And this was such an opportunity. However, explaining that to my children was another story. Jeff, Jr. and Christine were older now and had their own lives. Their father had moved into a one-bedroom apartment in Philadelphia, so he was readily available to them. Therefore, I didn't feel any pressing need to stay. After all, they could drive up to see us anytime.

Even though Jeff didn't outwardly protest, I suspected that he didn't like the idea of me moving to New York with Michelle. He knew that I could not resist such a great opportunity and that any protests from him would only diminish his chances of maintaining our already strained relationship. It was time I moved.

In a gesture of good faith, I allowed Jeff to spend New Year's Eve with me and the kids as we brought in the new millennium at my apartment. By the end of January, Michelle and I would be in a different state with a new life ahead of us.

***

The move was a positive step towards my recovery and healing. With it came a renewed sense of self worth and assurance that I could make a difference. My son and ex-husband accompanied us on moving day on our trek up north. They wanted to ensure our safe passage to the Promised Land. I felt like a newly-freed slave on an adventure in this brave new world.

Within one month of being transplanted, I traveled to San Francisco and Lake Tahoe and finally experienced a real ski trip. And this time I actually went skiing.

As I had done in previous years, the annual ritual of proclaiming resolutions and setting goals led me to start my own business as an independent beauty consultant. It was a great way to get beauty products at a discount, meet new people, and learn my way around the Island. I met my daughter's classmates, their parents, and some neighbors who became very good friends. These friends were a great support network for me as a newly single parent, and they offered to care for Michelle and to take her to and from after-school activities. Our transition was smooth, and Michelle's adjustment to her new surroundings was much better than my own.

During the summer, I went to Cancun with Rhoda and to Buffalo with Barbara and Marjorie, who had encouraged me to continue attending the networking conferences that had now become an annual ritual for us. In the coming years, I'd travel to several places around the country, and even to Puerto Rico. These trips might not seem important or worthwhile to you, but to someone who had long felt constrained, it was refreshing.

I allowed Jeff to visit and accompany us on Michelle's class canoe trip. She had asked if he would come, and I actually felt relieved when he said yes. I couldn't swim and was afraid of being out in the open waters alone with her. If anything would have happened to me, then he would be there. Jeff had made no concerted efforts to visit Michelle, and I was the one who initiated visits between the two by driving three hours to drop her off in Philadelphia so she could be with her father. His lack of initiation to establish and maintain regularly-scheduled visits only hurt him in the long run. I think I understood how painful it was for him to see me after the divorce, but I couldn't understand why he wouldn't venture out to see Michelle as often as he could. He had made a powerful bond with her since infancy, and I didn't want to see that bond broken because he and I were no longer together. But I guess that's one of the negative consequences of divorce -- a horrible tragedy that separates families.

I often reflected on how fortunate I was to have so many opportunities, and I was going to make the best of them. I was content. There was a sense of inner joy that I constantly possessed in spite of the problems, issues, trials, and turmoil I was going through with Jeff. I knew that the Lord was keeping me sane and it was through His strength that I was able to go on.

Just thinking about how wonderful God had been to me and how He delivered me out of the grips of sin and death would propel me into songs of praise. I would sing along with gospel music CD's or just sing aloud in the apartment to my favorite pop songs. Singing aloud made my heart soar. I continued reading empowering self-help books and found a couple of good local churches to attend. God had given me a second chance at life, and it was during these times of remembrance and thanksgiving that I rejoiced and imagined what heaven would be like in the presence of my Lord. Simply wonderful!

14
Reflection:
What Took Me So Long?

"When it becomes more difficult to suffer than to change…
you will change." – Dr. Robert Anthony

You have traveled with me this far on this journey and probably have a few nagging questions, such as, "What took you so long to leave?", "Why would you put up with it in the first place?", and "Why did you stay?" No doubt, you are thinking about how you would have handled the situation and how it would not have taken you as long as it took me. That's okay. We both have our histories and issues that come into play, and we both have our life's journey. Here's mine.

After I finally left the marriage and was on the outside looking in, I had those same questions, and I berated myself for enduring years of needless pain. I tried to understand what the purpose of it all was. I'll attempt to answer some of those questions in this chapter, as well as provide a deeper look into the "reflections" segments I used at the end of some of the chapters. I didn't want you to wait until the epilogue to deal with the painful issues presented.

There are several reasons why women stay in abusive relationships, and a lot of them have to do with our families of origin. I think that this is the most critical indicator of how a person copes with domestic abuse and other detrimental marital issues. What we learn during our childhood development stages goes far beyond young adulthood.

Family History

I grew up in a dysfunctional family. My father was an alcoholic, and my mother was asthmatic and used an inhaler. She was also codependent.

My father had three moods, one sober, one drunk, and one in the middle. When he was sober, nobody was happy because he was so irritable. When he was drunk, he was completely wasted and I remember several times when he would either fall down the stairs or fall asleep in his dinner plate. But, when he was in a mellow, slightly high mood, he was this nice and easy-going man who would sit down with me and show me how to draw, tell me stories about my infancy, and tell me how proud he was of me, his "slim goodie." Those instances were rare, but I favored those times the most.

My mother was efficient and organized, and our house was spotless. She'd have us clean the house inside and out every Saturday morning. When my father got paid every other Friday, she'd always go to his job and come back home with groceries. She'd call him in sick on the days he didn't go to work because he had a hangover. I didn't realize how unhappy my mother was until I was older and understood why she did some of the things she did. I remember one incident when she literally chased my father out of the house with a butcher knife in her hand. It was scary, but I had grown accustomed to the fighting between them.

I learned from watching my mother how to fix problems, how to keep the house neat and clean, and how to keep the children quiet. I learned how to not rock the boat or make waves and was a very compliant individual. I learned how to make excuses for my husband's actions, but I also learned how to keep him afloat and looking good and presentable to the outside world. This is also codependency.

I am an adult child of an alcoholic. Here is an explanation of "The Problem" as published by the Adult Children of Alcoholics World Service Organization, Inc.

> "Many of us found that we had several characteristics in common as a result of being brought up in alcoholic or other dysfunctional households.
>
> We had come to feel isolated and uneasy with other people, especially authority figures. To protect ourselves, we became people pleasers, even though we lost our own identities in the process. All the same we would mistake any personal criticism as a threat.
>
> We either became alcoholics ourselves, married them, or both. Failing that, we found other compulsive personalities, such as a workaholic, to fulfill our sick need for abandonment.
>
> We lived life from the standpoint of victims. Having an overdeveloped sense of responsibility, we preferred to be concerned with others rather than ourselves. We got guilt feelings when we trusted ourselves, giving in to others. We became reactors rather than actors, letting others take the initiative.
>
> We were dependent personalities, terrified of abandonment, willing to do almost anything to hold on to a relationship in order not to be abandoned emotionally. We keep choosing insecure relationships because they match our childhood relationship with alcoholic or dysfunctional parents.

These symptoms of the family disease of alcoholism or other dysfunction made us 'co-victims,' those who take on the characteristics of the disease without necessarily ever taking a drink. We learned to keep our feelings down as children and keep them buried as adults. As a result of this conditioning, we often confused love with pity, tending to love those we could rescue.

Even more self-defeating, we became addicted to excitement in all our affairs, preferring constant upset to workable solutions.

This is a description, not an indictment."

Low Self-Esteem

Low self esteem is another reason why I stayed. I was often teased while growing up. Kids can be cruel sometimes, and I was not immune to their scorn. They made fun of me because of my skin color, hair, the fact that I wore glasses, and my skinny body. I was called all kinds of names. By the time I reached sixteen, things started to change. I had decided to become funny and make people laugh with me instead of at me. I knew I was accepted by adults and teachers, but wanted to be accepted by my peers and developed a sense of humor to gain that acceptance. My mother was very good at encouraging me to stay true to myself and told me that the other kids were jealous because they weren't as smart as I was. I held on to her words, but I never got away from those feelings of inadequacy. I believe that's why I clung to the attention I got from Jeff.

Money

Another reason why I stayed was for financial security. I grew up in a low-income area of Philadelphia and was surrounded by poverty. Once I moved out and began to enjoy some of the luxuries of my hard work, I wasn't so eager to give it up. We had jobs, a house, two cars, and took family vacations. I knew that leaving Jeff would definitely change my lifestyle and significantly reduce my access to money. I had become accustomed to having nice things and going out to the movies and dinners, and I did not want to give up that way of living. Also, leaving Jeff would impact my ability to afford college for our children. I had always regretted not finishing college, and I wanted my children to have that opportunity and not to miss it for the lack of money.

Church

Our deep church involvement and good standing in the community were very important to me, and I wanted to maintain that status. I did not want the embarrassment of divorce or separation to come upon our family, and I feared being called a hypocrite. I was afraid of what people might say and was careful to present a perfect picture to the world. I wanted people to know that my Christian walk was upright and something to be admired. Unfortunately, some leaders in church ministry felt the same way and would not allow me to discuss my personal business with other congregation members. This only perpetuated the problem and allowed Jeff to continue in his offenses without reprimand or confrontation by others. Some of the people who did know what was going on kept their distance. They made only occasional or meager attempts to feed us with a long-handled spoon as though they might become infected with a disease. That response was very hurtful. But not too many people knew, especially since I kept it a secret until it became unbearable. During the period of secrecy, not even close church family and blood relatives knew of the pain, anger, hurt, and shame I was going through. However, toward the end, there were a handful of close friends and family members that I could depend on, and these wonderful individuals, Christian and non-Christian, helped to keep me afloat in the raging storm.

The Kids

And finally, I stayed for the sake of my children. I did not want my children to come from a broken home and be all messed up because their parents divorced. We were a Christian family and I believed that "the family that prays together, stays together." I didn't want us to be a statistic and tried very hard to keep the family intact.

I had always believed that the odds of divorce among Christian couples were pretty slim. And regarding divorce rates among Christian groups, Dr. Tom Ellis, chairman of the *Southern Baptist Convention's Council on the Family* said that for "...*born-again Christian couples who marry...in the church after having received premarital counseling...and attend church regularly and pray daily together...*" experience only 1 divorce out of nearly 39,000 marriages -- or 0.00256 percent.

But my marriage didn't qualify. We had not had the appropriate premarital counseling and had some serious issues to deal with. At times, Jeff would tell me to be quiet so that the kids would not hear us argue. And many times, I did keep quiet until, of course, I'd blow up in anger or deliver a scathing or sarcastic remark about something he had done that annoyed me. By then it was too late, and I could not pull back the words. I often wondered what the difference was between my verbal assaults compared to his physical assaults on my body. Probably not that much. The impact of both is still detrimental. By the time we divorced, my children had already come to accept that it was inevitable and had accepted my decision. One child even asked me, "What took you so long?"

***

So, now you want to know the point of all this. I've gone into lengthy detail about the beatings, betrayals, and unimaginable pains inflicted on me, but you wonder, "What's the point; what's the outcome, and why should we care?"

It's been years since I left Jeff and you'd think that by now I would have gotten over it. I have not gotten over the abuse. I sometimes still cry today when I think about how much of my life was wasted, but I realize that I went through all of this for a reason. I believe that God had a plan for me. I believe that He knew I could handle the turmoil without jumping off a bridge. I believe that God trusted me. It was either I believe that, or erroneously believe that I was being punished for some sin I had committed. I take solace in the fact that there was a divine reason for me to go through this period in my life and to tell the story that has been kept quiet for so long.

And the reason is this -- *One day, somewhere in this country, one woman, after reading my story, will leave her abuser for good just in time to be saved from serious injury or death!*

That's reason enough for me.

***

This next segment will address the unpleasant issues I had to face, along with facts and figures, as well as the steps I took to get away from my abuser. I'll use some of the notes from the end of chapter "Reflections" as a guide.

Chapter 1
Dating Violence

In 1974, when I met my husband, the term "dating violence" had not yet been invented, and I had no idea that our interactions were dysfunctional. Today, unfortunately, teen dating violence is considered less of a potential societal threat as compared to school violence and gang activity, and has not received the same level of community or national attention as researchers, advocates and teens would hope.

Teen dating violence is a pattern of actual or threatened acts of physical, sexual, and/or emotional abuse, perpetrated by an adolescent against a current or former dating partner. Abuse may include insults, coercion, social sabotage, sexual harassment, threats and/or acts of physical or sexual abuse. The abusive teen uses this pattern of violent and coercive behavior, in a heterosexual or homosexual dating relationship, in order to gain power and to maintain control over the dating partner.

A few statistics about dating violence:

- About one in three high school students have been or will be involved in an abusive relationship
- Forty percent of teenage girls ages 14 to 17 say they know someone their age who has been hit or beaten by a boyfriend
- One in five college females will experience some form of dating violence
- In a study of 500 young women, ages 15 to 24, it was found that 60 percent were currently involved in an ongoing abusive relationship and that all participants had experienced violence in a dating relationship
- Six out of 10 rapes of young women occur in their own home or a friend or relative's home, not in a dark alley

Teenagers can choose better relationships when they learn to identify the early warning signs, understand that they have choices, and believe that they are valuable people who deserve to be treated with respect. The teen should talk to a trusted adult or locate a shelter or agency to help make a plan to end the relationship and to remain safe in the process.

Post-Abortion Syndrome

Post-Abortion Syndrome (PAS) is a term that has been used to describe the emotional and psychological consequences of abortion. Whenever we go through a traumatic experience without the opportunity to process the experience emotionally, we can expect a delayed negative reaction. We live in a society that ignores the painful consequences of abortion. Men and women who have experienced it are urged into denial, so they do not talk about and process the normal feelings of anxiety, fear, shame, guilt, and grief which often follow the abortion. When such emotions are denied and buried, they will often resurface, having been magnified by time.

Some of the symptoms of PAS include guilt, anger, anxiety, broken relationships, depressions, sense of loss, suicide, and psychological "numbing." I struggled with guilt, and my inner voice of self-condemnation repeated a tape day in and day out. I believed that many of the unpleasant events I experienced were inevitable because I "deserved it."

Chapter 2

The marriage relationship should be based on equality, not on power and control. Some of the characteristics of a successful marriage are:

- Trust and support
- Mutual respect
- Non-threatening behavior
- Negotiation and fairness
- Economic partnership

- Shared responsibility
- Responsible parenting
- Honesty and accountability

Chapter 3
Domestic Abuse

The National Coalition Against Domestic Violence (NCADV) describes battering as a pattern of behavior used to establish power and control over another person with whom an intimate relationship is or has been shared through fear and intimidation, often including the threat or use of violence. Battering happens when one person believes that he or she is entitled to control another.

Some of the characteristics of domestic abuse include:

1. Emotional/psychological abuse
2. Isolation
3. Using children
4. Intimidation
5. Economic/financial abuse
6. Male privilege
7. Coercion and threats
8. Minimizing, denying and blaming
9. Physical violence
10. Forced sexual contact or sexual violence

Some horrifying facts about domestic violence are listed below, and an exhaustive list can be found on the NCADV website:

- One in every four women will experience domestic violence in their lifetimes.
- Almost one-third of female homicide victims that are reported in police records are killed by an intimate partner.
- Sexual assault or forced sex occurs in approximately 40-45% of battering relationships.

- The cost of intimate partner violence exceeds $5.8 billion each year. $4.1 billion of which is for direct medical and mental health services.
- Witnessing violence between one's parents or caretakers is the strongest risk factor of transmitting violent behavior from one generation to the next.
- An estimated 1.3 million women are victims of physical assault by an intimate partner each year.
- Nearly 7.8 million women have been raped by an intimate partner at some point in their lives.
- Most cases of domestic violence are never reported to the police.

If you are reading this and realize you're in an abusive relationship, STOP! Call the National Domestic Violence Hotline 1-800-799-SAFE (7233) and get help.

Adultery

There can be healing after a devastating affair. However, both parties will need to go to marital counseling and individual therapy, and the offending party will have to make significant lifestyle changes and be willing to undergo the restoration process. It is very bad if the offending party refuses to go through the process or makes excuses and blames others. I recommend reading *The Truth about Cheating - Why Men Stray and What You Can Do to Prevent It*, by M. Gary Neuman.

Chapter 6

I was exhausted from all the years of emotional, psychological, and physical abuse and was on the verge of being killed a couple of times. I always knew God kept me alive, but sometimes wondered what kept me going. So, the question could have easily been, "Is she dead yet?" after having gone through the five deadly adversaries of marriage: abortion, adultery, addiction, alcohol, and abuse.

Chapter 8
Drug Addiction

I was totally off guard and never suspected my husband was using crack cocaine until it was much too late. However, today there is abundant information on the Internet about crack cocaine addiction. The crack addict often:

- Changes his or her circle of friends and withdrawals from non-using family and friends
- Borrows or steals money to buy the drug
- Compulsively seeks crack and dwells on the next use
- Experiences personality changes, poor judgment, and loss of interest in previously enjoyable activities
- Becomes evasive or lies about activities or whereabouts

Chapter 12
Stalking

Stalking is a course of conduct directed at a specific person that would cause a reasonable person to feel fear. Even though I only recall being stalked once by Jeff, it was a terrifying event. This is a serious crime, a felony in some states, that many people underestimate. Here are some facts and figures to prove it:

- 76% of intimate partner female homicide victims have been stalked by their intimate partner
- 81% of women stalked by a current or former intimate partner are also physically assaulted by that partner; 30% are also sexually assaulted by that partner
- 54% of female homicide victims reported stalking to police before they were killed by their stalkers
- 30% of stalking victims are stalked by a current or former intimate partner

It's important to know how to protect yourself against a stalker. Linden Gross published 10 measures that may save your life if you're being stalked:

1. Avoid all contact.
2. Don't react to the stalker.
3. Withdraw gently.
4. Get a new unlisted phone number and private post office box.
5. Carry a cell phone with you for safety.
6. Protect your house.
7. Change your routes and routines.
8. Inform others.
9. Paper never stops bullets.
10. Consider moving – it might just save your life.

I didn't have a lot of resources during the time I was going through all this. Federal, state and local laws had not yet taken up the mantle to help battered women, and very little was known about the number and severity of those affected by domestic abuse. The Internet had not yet been invented and resources were limited. I had to develop a few tactics of my own, and here's a list of the some of the things I did to break free and to stay free:

1. Left the abuser
2. Got a protection from abuse order
3. Got medical attention
4. Got counseling and psychotherapy
5. Got a divorce
6. Surrounded myself with loving family and friends for support and prayer
7. Took care of myself and did things I enjoyed
8. Developed new skills for healthy relationships
9. Prayed for myself and asked God to change me

***

Now, let's get back to this story and get you to the surprise ending.

15
Residual Effects

"Life is a roller coaster. You can either scream every time you hit a bump or you can throw your hands up in the air and enjoy it." – Author Unknown

"For I am persuaded, that neither death, nor life, nor angels, nor principalities, nor powers, nor things present, nor things to come, Nor height, nor depth, nor any other creature, shall be able to separate us from the love of God, which is in Christ Jesus our Lord." – Romans 8:38-39

Four years later.

I was just drifting off to sleep around 11 o'clock one cold Friday night in January 2004 when the phone rang. It was my daughter Christine. I could hear the anxiety in her voice as she fought back the tears trying to tell me that her father was gone. Not willing to be drawn back in the fray, I said that it wasn't my turn to watch him. With sympathy to her plight, I reassured her that her dad was okay wherever he was and that he'd turn up in a couple of days. I had remembered his disappearing acts from times past and was annoyed that he was pulling this stunt now and causing those closest to him to panic and feel helpless.

She repeated, "Mom, he's gone."

And again I said, "I'm sorry, Honey, but don't worry. He'll show up in a couple of days."

I was disappointed that he had started using cocaine again and that his adult children and his current girlfriend were wrapped up in his addiction. I had wished they weren't codependent like I had been. Then she started to sob. And, that's when I knew what she really meant. He really was gone, and this time he wasn't coming back.

I packed an overnight bag as quickly as I could. I aroused Michelle and told her to get dressed and that we had to leave right away to see her dad. I lied and said that he was very sick. She lumbered into the back seat of the car and was grateful for the pillow and blanket I had provided so she could sleep on the ride down. A little over three hours later we arrived at the hospital lobby where Jeff, Jr. and Christine were waiting. Immediately, the children embraced, and Jeff, Jr. clenched his little sister tightly as he explained to her that their father had died. We all needed to be together now. We took the elevator up, and Jeff, Jr. and Christine went ahead into the room and stood at their father's bedside. Pastor Al and his wife Maxine, and Jeff's girlfriend were already assembled in the room.

I clung to my little girl as we walked slowly down the hall. I could smell the familiar aroma of hand sanitizer and disinfectant. The smell reminded me of the last visit I had with my father who died from throat cancer, with my grandfather who died from prostate cancer two years earlier, and of other loved ones who never left the hospital alive. As we approached, I heard the beeps from hospital monitors in adjacent rooms and the faint whispers coming from Jeff's room. I was overwhelmed and couldn't go any further. My legs gave way, and I crumbled to the floor pulling my daughter down with me. We held on to each other and cried. Our sobs echoed down the hall. I didn't want to wake any of the other patients by reminding them that the hospital is also a place of death, but I couldn't help myself. I couldn't get my legs to respond, and I couldn't stop the tears. I just couldn't get up. My heart was broken. The man I had loved for so long was dead. My son and Pastor Al rushed out into the hall, scooped us off the floor, and ushered us into the room.

Last fall, Michelle had mistakenly spilled the beans and told me that her dad's twenty-something-year-old girlfriend was pregnant and that the baby was expected around Christmas. Jeff had instructed the kids not to tell me about the pregnancy. I wasn't as upset as maybe he thought I might be. Surprised, but not upset. I thought, finally, he would stop asking me about getting back together and we'd stop having those same arguments about reconciliation.

I remember one conversation when he asked about getting back together and I told him no. He said in a defeated tone that maybe he should just go ahead and give his girlfriend the ring. I encouraged him to do so and hoped that that would have been the beginning of him rebuilding his life. Him having a baby seemed to signal his recovery and solidify his desire to start over. At least that's what I had hoped. Inwardly, though, I sympathized with any woman who would have to live with him if he wasn't emotionally well or if he was still using drugs. So, whenever I had asked the children about how his girlfriend was doing, it wasn't because I was jealous, nosy, or envious in any way. I just wanted to make sure she wasn't being abused by him. I wanted the children to be on the lookout for any telltale signs of domestic violence, such as social withdrawal or unexplained bruises on her. I don't think they believed I had her best interests at heart, and who could blame them? I believed that they told me she was fine just to stop my questioning, but I had my doubts. However, my suspicions were never confirmed.

Jeff had called us in November to announce that he had recently been cured of liver cancer. I was skeptical about his declaration and asked him if he wasn't sure the true diagnosis was cirrhosis of the liver. He brushed off my comment and asked if I were happy about his medical miracle. I was alerted awhile back by the children that he was in the hospital for a stomach condition but was never led to believe it was anything as serious as cancer. I had called his eldest brother and sister and told them that he was in the hospital. I realized the importance of his family's support, but Jeff didn't want his family to know and had not previously told them of his illness. My concern for Jeff was still evident after all these years.

I had come to learn over the years that some of Jeff's family didn't like me. Some demonstrated their disregard for me and our marriage by giving Jeff money for drugs, housing him, and allowing him to bring various women around them. Some of his family members were angry with me, and I'm sure they blamed me for a lot of Jeff's troubles. I understood that and had accepted it. They loved their brother very much and would do anything to make him happy and to help ease his pain. Some of them were caught up in the same codependent cycle that I had been. But they had only heard one side of the story and didn't know the whole truth. The side they heard was from a bitter and broken man whose life was completely changed when he allowed alcohol and drug abuse, illicit sex, and violence take over his life. My decision to leave him was based on my desire to live pain-free.

There were also a few of Jeff's family members who did like me, and they understood my plight. I carry their care and love for me in my heart and appreciate the measures they took to show that they were concerned.

The kids had often visited their father and it appeared that their relationship was improving. He was close by and had given them advice, money, food, and a place of refuge whenever their lives were a little chaotic or out of sorts. I was glad that he was there for them. I knew that my move to New York had forced them to grow up a lot quicker than if I had stayed. I was very grateful that Jeff was available for them and it seemed like he was getting better. But I later found out that my older children had been silent about his bouts with alcohol and drugs and that he had temporarily lost his driver's license because of a DUI charge. I was saddened that they were exhibiting codependent tendencies.

At Christmastime, I had allowed Michelle to visit Jeff so that she would be there when the baby arrived. The baby boy was born just before the New Year. A few days later, Michelle came back home, and Jeff caught the flu. Jeff, Jr. had visited his dad on a Wednesday and encouraged him to go to the doctor. He was coughing up blood. Jeff's girlfriend took him to the hospital on Thursday evening and within 24 hours he was dead. Apparently, the blood vessels in his esophagus had burst, and he drowned in his own blood. It's called esophageal asphyxiation. The autopsy report revealed that he died from massive gastrointestinal hemorrhaging, secondary to hepatitis C, cirrhosis, and alcohol abuse. He was only 48 years old.

Jeff was alone when he died that cold Friday night. His girlfriend had not called his children when he was admitted into the hospital, and as far as I know, no one else knew he was hospitalized. She was at another hospital caring for her newborn son who was under observation with some obscure scalp infection. Jeff died with no one by his side. No one was there to pray with him. No one was there to pray for him. No one was there to hold his hand or to give him comfort during his last hours. He didn't deserve to die so horribly.

As Michelle and I were scooped to our feet and led into the room, I wiped my eyes, went over to the bed, and rested my hand on his lifeless chest. I remembered how virile and attractive he used to be and now his body was swollen and stiff. I glanced at his girlfriend as she sat in the chair on the other side of the bed. I avoided direct eye contact with her because I was afraid of expressing the hurt and anger I started to feel towards her for allowing Jeff's health to get so bad. I didn't want to engage in any conversation with her, but I gave her a passive greeting.

I then took command of the room as I examined Jeff's body for myself. I walked around to the foot of the bed, lifted the sheet to look at his feet, exclaimed that the liver spots were a telltale sign of liver disease, and demanded to know from those present why no one had realized that. It was as plain as day that he was very sick. Why didn't anyone tell me? I yelled into the air again and again and screamed for someone to tell me why I wasn't told that he was in the hospital and that he was so sick. No one answered my screams. No one answered my cries for an explanation. Maybe no one heard me. Maybe no one could hear me screaming at the top of my lungs. They couldn't hear me, because I hadn't opened my mouth. I didn't want to wake the other patients.

I turned and rushed into my son's arms. I started to cry. With muffled sobs, I slumped into my son's chest clutching him as hard as I could.

Jeff may have had many problems with alcohol and drug use, anger, and control issues, but he didn't deserve to die like this. He may have been quite harsh at times, but why did he have to die like this, all alone, without his children, his siblings, or me by his side as he left this world? I was angry that his girlfriend did not have the decency to call anybody to see about Jeff – not even his own kids.

***

The next few days were somber, and Jeff's sudden death shocked both our families and all of our friends. Our children had no warning and were not prepared to bury their father either emotionally or financially. Jeff had not left a will or life insurance policy and had no savings. He did tell me once that he had a $10,000 death rider benefit on a medical insurance policy and that he had named his girlfriend as beneficiary. I asked him why he hadn't listed his children as beneficiaries since he wasn't married. He had no answer. I told him that that decision had disturbed me and was a bad move on his part, but it was his choice, and I couldn't argue with that.

The patriarch of Jeff's family called a meeting to raise funds to pay for the funeral. I had no financial obligation to pay for his funeral, since we were divorced, but that didn't stop me from giving my children money and helping them make funeral arrangements. However, they had to make crucial decisions by themselves. I put them in touch with the administration of Deliverance Evangelistic Church. Deliverance was the church where Jeff got saved back in 1975. The church helped Christine and Jeff, Jr. with the funeral arrangements. I was gratified that we were able to have his home going service at the place where Jeff's Christian life began. I thought it was appropriate to end his earthly walk with the Lord at the place where he spent so much of his early years in ministry. And his final resting place would be within a few yards of his parents' gravesite. Now it was time to say goodbye.

***

Friends started to gather in the chapel lobby. Some chatted quietly while others stood in line to sign the guest registry or were already seated in the chapel. People I had not seen in years greeted me with hugs, kisses, and condolences and commented on how shocking it was to hear that Jeff died.

A modestly dressed elderly woman walked towards me and reached for my hands. "Lawanna?" she asked already knowing the answer. She smiled as though she was keeping a wonderful secret and couldn't wait to let it out. Her eyes glistened, and her creamy smooth skin did not reveal her true age.

I said, "Hello," as I gazed upon the sweet face of this beautiful and gentle woman.

"You don't remember me do you?" she quizzed.

"Oh, ma'am, your voice is so familiar. Please keep talking and it'll come to me," I said as I squeezed and rocked her hands in mine.

"It's Maxine," she whispered as she finally let the cat out of the bag.

"Maxine Barfield?" Tears welled up in my eyes and a flood of lovely memories came to mind. I hugged her, kissed her cheek and squealed with delight. I recalled how we met at work back in 1976. The lunches we shared and the friendship we made. I hadn't seen or spoken to Maxine since I moved away. I remembered the many questions she had about Christianity, and there she was some 28 years later. She told that she had read about Jeff's death in the church bulletin and made plans to come to the chapel to see me but that she could not stay for the services. I was happy to see her and even more thrilled that she was still enjoying her walk with God. I only wished that I had not lost contact with her all those years.

One of Jeff's best friends whom I had not seen in over 14 years hugged me tightly. Again, the flood gates of my eyes and mind opened wide. All the good memories came to me and an inner peace surrounded the place where we were. Even in the midst of a funeral the love of family and friends kept me warm and safe.

I didn't feel awkward sitting beside my children as the mourners greeted us as they passed his body in the casket. I was quite comfortable in church and had been at Jeff's side for more than 25 years. Now was no different, except that he just wasn't sitting next to me talking about how the message had affected him. I felt as though he was just sleeping. I didn't feel that sense of dread and fear of not ever seeing him again. I was confident and believed with all my heart that he was with the Lord regardless of his faults, frailties, and hang-ups. Some people in the sanctuary that day understood and shared that same sense of peace and assurance.

The struggles that Jeff and I had as a couple left me stronger and resilient. I felt a great sense of accomplishment as I stood with my children whole and not broken by the effects of an abusive marriage. People greeted me throughout the day telling me how radiant and wonderful I looked. Those compliments only solidified the fact that being separated from Jeff was a good thing for me, both physically and emotionally. I recalled looking at old photos of myself where I looked haggard and worn down. I saw the sadness in my eyes and was thankful that the real me had finally emerged.

As I watched my son at the podium recounting fond memories of his father, all I could think about was how difficult life would be for him. He would never be able to reconcile with his father in true love, acceptance, and forgiveness. Christine and Michelle sat in the back pew for a few moments cradling their new baby brother with all the love they had. I knew they wanted more than ever to have anything they could get of their father and this was the perfect time to bond and be close to one another. My daughters loved that precious baby boy who would never know their father. But there was still so much healing that needed to occur.

I had forgiven Jeff a long time ago and was very sorry that he would not be around for his children or to ever see any grandchildren. I was heartbroken for my children who would miss their father terribly and who probably feel just as lost now as they had when we divorced. But I couldn't help that. All I could do was pray for them and be with them as much as I could. Unfortunately, they would have to navigate this journey of life and death for themselves.

And as life does go on, challenges come to make us stronger and wiser. Little did we know that a new challenge was lurking just around the corner.

Epilogue

We sat quietly in the small holding cell wondering how in the world we got there. The locked room had only the essentials -- two steel benches screwed against graffiti-marked walls, a broken pay phone, and the darkened and scratched Plexiglas one-way mirror. If you peered closely enough at the mirror you could see a security camera on the other side in an adjacent room. I imagined that the room where we sat had held criminals who were on their way to prison, as well as innocent people who were at the wrong place at the wrong time and were wrongly accused. But why were we here? We weren't criminals. We were accused of a crime that didn't even happen. Christine sucked her teeth and pursed her lips in disgust. Jeffery, Jr. sulked. I tried to make light of the situation and reassured my children that this misunderstanding would soon be over.

Keys rattled, an officer appeared, and we were called one-by-one to be processed. I confirmed my identity as listed on my driver's license. I followed the state trooper and stood against the wall as instructed. I turned left and could hear the click of the digital camera. I turned right. Another click. When I turned to face the officer for my final snapshot, I almost smiled. I had to remind myself that this wasn't a photo shoot for a glamour magazine cover story or a photo for the family album. However, my active imagination couldn't help but wander as my fingertips were rolled onto the black ink pad and pressed into little squares on a piece of paper. I thought,

"So this is what it feels like to be locked up." I thought of Rosa Parks, Martin Luther King, Jr., and Nelson Mandela.

As my subconscious mind continued on autopilot, I recalled going to the apartment that Jeff shared with his girlfriend the day after he died. As I walked through accessible rooms of the apartment I saw the old knick knacks and artwork I had picked out from years past, our old bedroom set, the old family Bible that Jeff had bargained for, and other treasures from our married life together. Now that he was gone, I just assumed she'd return those items to his children. I had counted them lost to me when I moved out of our home, but these precious items still held value to our children and rightfully belonged to them. A few weeks later, I found out that she had intended to keep everything that was in that apartment. And that's how the trouble started.

I was back in New York after the funeral when I got a call from Jeff's relative with whom I had never spoken. So I was quite surprised when he called me to make small talk, telling me how good I looked and what not. I was suspicious of his call and wondered what he was up to. He asked me about Jeff's stereo system. "Aha! So that's what this is all about," I thought as my suspicions were confirmed. I told him that Jeff's children had all legal rights to those items from their childhood and that the girlfriend only had rights to those items she purchased with Jeff when they lived together. There was silence on the other end of the phone. I went on and reminded him that Jeff, Jr. and Christine were the legal and rightful heirs to everything in that apartment that belonged to their father prior to his relationship with his new girlfriend. I told him that I was prepared to make sure my children were not denied this right and that I would take this matter to court if necessary. I couldn't stress this enough, and the tone of my voice grew increasingly loud and intense with every word. How dare she take anything from my children. I was seething.

A few days later, Christine received a call from her father's girlfriend that she and Jeff, Jr. could come and get whatever items they wanted. My kids asked me for money to rent a small truck. I drove down, gave them the money, and went back to upstate New York. That afternoon they provided identification to the landlord and were given access to enter the apartment. Christine and Jeff, Jr. did not have a key to the apartment, and the girlfriend was not present. They only had the truck for a few hours and loaded only those items that were previously agreed upon between them and the girlfriend.

Afterwards, Christine and Michelle drove to attend the baby shower that Jeff's family had put together for their father's infant son. However, when Christine complained about the girlfriend's absence at the apartment when she had made prior arrangements to be there as agreed, the family cursed my daughters and sent them out of the house crying. Later that afternoon, unbeknownst to us, Jeff's family accompanied the girlfriend back to the apartment, called the state police, and filed a report.

Within days, I received a warrant for my arrest in the mail and was ordered to appear at the Delaware State Police Station for processing on a specified date. Christine and Jeffery also received letters for their arrest. We were charged with criminal trespass in the first degree, and it seemed to carry a sentence of 150 years in prison. Well, not quite 150 years. Fortunately, my 14 year-old daughter was spared the humiliation. I often wondered why the family did not have my 14 year-old daughter charged with criminal trespass. Were they trying to be kind to her?

So, here we were getting our mug shots. After the paperwork, we returned to the holding area until called by the judge via videoconferencing. We were released on our own recognizance and ordered to appear for a hearing at some later date. Within weeks, my son's attorney was able to get our cases dismissed but the damage had already been done.

The criminal records were on file and would appear whenever my children applied for jobs or houses or land for the rest of their lives until they could afford to have those records expunged. To this day, my children are still hurt that some of their so-called family members conspired and initiated such an injustice against them. They also have mixed feelings about the girlfriend having moved across the country with her infant son without a forwarding address. Maybe my children will get to meet their younger brother one day. Maybe our family will recover from the damaging effects of domestic violence and get to experience mutual love that is based on equality and nonviolence. But that will be another story.

Bibliography / Recommended Reading

"Dating Violence" (Date Unknown). Available from: The Alabama Coalition Against Domestic Violence <http://www.acadv.org/dating.html> (accessed 10 September 2009).

"Domestic Violence and Abuse – Warning Signs and Symptoms of Abusive Relationships" (2001). Available from: Helpguide.org <http://www.helpguide.org/mental/domestic_violence_abuse_types_signs_causes_effects.htm> (accessed 26 June 2009).

"Domestic Violence and Abuse: Help, Treatment, Intervention, and Prevention" (2001). Available from: Helpguide.org <http://www.helpguide.org/mental/domestic_violence_abuse_help_treatment_prevention.htm> (accessed 15 July 2009).

"Domestic Violence Facts" (2007). Available from: National Coalition Against Domestic Violence <http://www.ncadv.org/files/DomesticViolenceFactSheet(National).pdf> (accessed 6 December 2008).

"Effects of Crack Cocaine Use and Crack Addiction Treatment Information" (2005). Available from: eGetgoing, Inc. <http://www.egetgoing.com/drug_rehab/crack_cocaine.asp> (accessed 10 September 2009).

Gray, John. *Men are from Mars, women are from Venus a practical guide for improving communication and getting what you want in your relationships.* New York, NY: HarperCollins, 1992.

Gross, Linden. "If You're Being Stalked Here are 10 Measures That May Save Your Life" (2003). Available from: Stalking Victims Sanctuary <http://www.stalkingvictims.com/survival/pdfs/10_measures.pdf> (accessed 12 September 2009).

Hall, Laurie. *An Affair of the Mind.* Colorado Springs, CO: Focus on the Family Publishing, 1996.

Holy Bible. Nashville: Thomas Nelson, 1975.

Jeffers, Susan. *Feel the Fear and Do It Anyway.* New York: Fawcett Columbine, 1987.

Meyer, Joyce. *Battlefield of the Mind: Winning the Battle in Your Mind.* New York, NY: Faith Words, 1995.

Neuman, M. Gary. *The Truth about Cheating – Why Men Stray and What You Can Do to Prevent It.* Hoboken, NJ: John Wiley & Sons, Inc., 2008.

Owen, Catherine. "Crack Cocaine Addiction" (2007). Available from: Suite101.com <http://drug-abuse.suite101.com/print_article.cfm/crack_cocaine_addiction> (accessed 8 August 2009).

"Physical and Psychological Complications of Abortion – Part 1: Post-Abortion Syndrome" (1995). Available from: Leadership U <http://www.leaderu.com/orgs/tul/papl.html> (accessed 10 September 2009).

"The Problem" (Date Unknown). Available from: Adult Children of Alcoholics World Service Organization, Inc. <http://www.adultchildren.org/lit/Problem.s> (accessed 10 September 2009).

"The Problem: What is Battering" (2005). Available from: National Coalition Against Domestic Violence <http://www.ncadv.org/learn/TheProblem.php> (accessed 21 March 2008).

"Stalking Fact Sheet" (2009). Available from: Stalking Resource Center <http://www.ncvc.org/src> (accessed 12 September 2009).

"Teen Dating Violence – Overview" (2004). Available from: National Resource Center on Domestic Violence < http://new.vawnet.org/Assoc_Files_VAWnet/NRC_TDV-Overview.pdf> (accessed 10 September 2009).

"Teen Power & Control Wheel" (Date Unknown). Available from: The Alabama Coalition Against Domestic Violence <http://www.acadv.org/teenpcwheel.html> (accessed 10 September 2009).

"U.S. divorce rates for various faith groups, age groups, & geographic areas" (2000). Available from: Religious Tolerance <http://www.religioustolerance.org/chr_dir.htm> (accessed 12 September 2009).

About the Author

Lawanna Lynn Campbell is a survivor of domestic violence. She graduated third in her high school class of more than 500 students and received a full Academic Meritorious Scholarship to attend Temple University in Philadelphia. She works full-time as a legal assistant for a staffing company and is a volunteer instructor and presenter with the American Red Cross. Her vibrant personality, quick-witted humor, and extraordinary storytelling skills will leave an indelible imprint on your heart. She has three adult children, lives on Long Island in New York and is engaged to be married.

For more information visit www.isshedeadyet.com.

Breinigsville, PA USA
24 January 2010
231254BV00001B/1/P